YESTERDAY'S
CHILDREN

YESTERDAY'S CHILDREN

The Extraordinary Search
for my
PAST LIFE FAMILY

Jenny Cockell

PIATKUS

© 1993 Jenny Cockell

First published in 1993 by
Judy Piatkus (Publishers) Ltd of
5 Windmill Street, London W1P 1HF

The moral right of the author has been asserted

A catalogue record for this book is
available from the British Library

ISBN 0−7499−1246−4

Edited by Susan Fleming
Designed by Sue Ryall

Set in Compugraphic Plantin by
Action Typesetting Limited, Gloucester
Printed and bound in Great Britain by
Butler & Tanner Ltd, Frome

Certain names have been changed in order to protect family members and various other people who might prefer not to be associated with the subject of this book.

Contents

Introduction

Mary died twenty-one years before I was born but memories of her life and of that time were always a part of me, shaping and affecting the person I grew to become. This is an account of the search both for the children Mary left behind and for self-understanding; through reaching out to the past I had to unearth and face my own feelings of inadequacy and fear and find the reasons behind these emotions. I knew that I had to try to find the children 'of yesterday' or my life would always be shadowed by memories of the past, of grief, anger and loss. In part, this book is written to and for Mary's children.

Before the search could begin I needed to develop the courage and strength to pursue my dreams. I could never be certain that a satisfactory conclusion would be achieved and I was constantly dogged with doubts and uncertainties. The road was never going to be easy. I was driven by obsession towards a goal that, deep inside, I knew was there to be reached if only enough effort was made, for long enough and in the right direction.

Even the process of sharing this story seemed to have a

place in the experience as a whole. Seeking the opinions of others and gauging feeling has helped me to meet my need for approval and find out how others view what I see as the memory of my previous life. I had always been puzzled that others seemed unable to remember any of their other lives, and at times I found it hard to believe that they could not. Writing this book has helped me to find out why *my* normality was not the normality experienced by others.

It's hard to be certain where my story starts — it's not really with my childhood or even my birth. In a sense it starts with Mary's death. But of one thing I am sure, it would never have happened without the dream . . .

1

A Jigsaw of Past Life Memories

In childhood, my dreams were swamped by memories of Mary's death. As Mary, I was in a large room with white walls; a tall, multi-paned window, almost opposite me, let in a great deal of light. I knew that I had been ill for a little while, possibly weeks, but by now the physical pain had become remote. I had difficulty breathing, though, and had to make an effort to draw each breath, which in itself induced panic. There was also a fever which brought with it a distortion of thought and of perceived time. The only certainty was that I was alone and near death in a place that was not home.

All this, however, seemed inconsequential beside my fear for the children I was leaving behind. The thought that I was being wrenched away from them made me want to try to fight the inescapable death, to try to avoid that final separation, even whilst knowing the futility of the fight. For death did come, inevitably and repeatedly, through those dreams.

I would wake in tears, sobbing with anger. But I was a withdrawn and nervous child, so I cried quietly and alone, too afraid to call for my mother to comfort me, and fearing punishment from my father. I was alone with my pain as Mary was alone in death in the dreams. Later, during daylight hours, I might tell my mother a little of Mary and my dreams, but I could not begin to unburden myself of the sense of grief trapped within me, and which remained. It was not death itself that animated my fear, for through the dreams I had come to understand death as a normal, natural process. It was the grief and loss *through* death that caused the tears. It was too soon to go, much too soon to leave the children.

I also felt in some way that it was my fault, a feeling that I was unable to discuss, for one of the strongest emotions I remember was a sense of guilt. I knew that I had escaped from a bad situation, but in doing so had left the children on their own. It was a release not sought, but forced upon me, yet the sense of guilt and responsibility remained. I was only a child, but my mind was dominated by a confusion of emotions that would have been difficult even for an adult to cope with.

These night-time dreams were bad, but I was able to recall other times in Mary's life, usually during the daytime. Many of these thoughts were more pleasant.

The strongest memories were of the children. I could remember an older son who was getting quite tall and may have been as old as thirteen. He was a little soldier, confident, very open and straightforward, a good judge of situations and not afraid of being gentle. The oldest girl was rather quiet at times; she had long hair and a thick fringe. This daughter was very patient, willing and helpful – I remembered her going to fetch water from a pump or a spring – and I knew she was clever, doing well at school. I felt particularly guilty for her, since she would be forced to look after the others, as girls are always expected to do. She would not be able to deal with the housework and the young ones, and do her school work.

Then there were at least a couple of boys, the elder of whom was energetic and had a relentless sense of humour; a slightly younger boy who fell in with him, or as often as not fell out and argued, was quieter and perhaps a little secretive. A younger girl, whom I felt was no more than five, was very pretty and blonde with blue eyes and a strongly feminine personality. And there was a very small boy who ran his hand absent-mindedly along the hem of his jacket, fidgeting with his clothes; he was a little uncomfortable, very quiet, a little remote, something of a loner. I felt he was a child one could not help but like, but who was uneasy about too much affection. I remembered wanting to hug him, but knowing he would feel smothered by such demonstrativeness.

When Mary died, I felt that there was one younger child and that there were seven or eight of them in all, but I was not confident about the details. I seem, for some reason, to have remembered one blonde child particularly, for my favourite childhood doll had slightly curly, sandy blonde hair. She had an ingenious mechanism which enabled her eyes to change colour, but I always kept them at blue. Essentially a baby doll, she has remained in my possession, dressed in baby clothes, to this day.

Other strong memories were of the cottage and walking along the lane next to it. The cottage was the first on the left on a quiet westward lane and stood sideways, close to the road edge and separated from it by a stone wall. This was not too high to see over but was uncomfortable to lean on; there were perhaps stones on edge placed along the top, and possibly plants that prevented one from getting too close to it on the cottage side. There was a gateway opening a little way in front of the cottage; it was quite large – perhaps a farm gateway. There may have been some sort of track from the gate in addition to the well-worn pathway running through the field to the cottage.

The building was of buff colour stone, though I felt that it should have been painted white; I seem to remember both. Above the solid-looking wooden door, the roof, which did not look thatched but was perhaps slate, sagged noticeably.

The cottage was small – certainly not very deep front to back. The few small windows did not let in much light and seemed to be mainly at the front; there were none at the gable end near the road. Just inside the door and directly ahead was some sort of wooden partition that made it impossible to walk straight in; you had to turn to one side or the other of the partition. There were no stairs, so I assumed the cottage was single-storey, and although there were very few rooms I do remember a few small attached outbuildings.

The kitchen seemed to run the depth of the cottage front to back, and was very cramped and quite dark. The details inside were vague, but I think there was a picture of a soldier on the wall. There was also some sort of furniture, a table against the wall and other things – nothing ornate, just functional.

Mary spent much of her time in the kitchen cooking, which seemed to involve a lot of boiling on something completely unfamiliar to me as a child – a kitchen range of a type that I did not see until adulthood and may still be found in some old houses. She also frequently made a round flat loaf of bread, mixing flour with her hands. I would echo this in childhood play, mixing grass seeds with water.

Further facets of that other life were acted out in my own daily life as a child. I kept our garden shed clean, sweeping the wooden floor with a broom just as Mary would sweep her hard stone floor. My mother had a vacuum cleaner and rarely used a broom, but I would enjoy cleaning in that older way, without machines. Neither was it a game – the job would be performed in reality and thoroughly, even when I was quite young. I was also constantly tidying and clearing out my room and toys, something that I enjoyed almost more than playing with them.

Before you got to the wall by the cottage, the left side of the road was fringed with trees and a hedgerow. The cottage itself had to be passed before reaching the entrance, so you then had to turn and walk back across the field to it. To the rear, beyond a small vegetable patch, was woodland. Further along the lane past the cottage entrance was a stream, which crossed the lane under a bridge. Mary's cottage marked the beginning of a small hamlet of perhaps ten to twelve homes, mainly strung along the same side of the lane. Though there was one house a bit further along, on the other side by a right-hand turning, most of the opposite side of the lane consisted of boggy meadows not suitable for building on.

The nearby village I remember in detail. All travel to and from it was done on foot; as Mary, I remember walking with the children to church, and alone when going shopping. Most of the shops stood on a north-to-south road in the middle of the village, where there was also a small church. From this road it was possible to see a large pair of wooden gates on the opposite side of the main road and to the right of the junction; these had some significance. The railway station was set back from the main road, which ran along the top of the village in an arc. Mary had some interest in steam trains and I often dreamed about them, but I cannot remember travelling on them. I knew the village to be north of a major city that was perhaps too far to walk to. The village of Mary's childhood I also felt to be fairly near, for I knew somehow that she had moved to this area from somewhere else.

I was fairly good at drawing as a child, and would repeatedly draw rough maps of Mary's village, marking the shops, the main roads, the station and her home. Sometimes other remembered landmarks would appear, but there was a remarkable consistency throughout the years.

Although there were occasional trips into the city (without the children) and others in the opposite direction — turning left out of the cottage — the main outings were to church. At least I presumed that they were to church, because everyone was present and dressed in garments that were not working clothes. (I always felt that Mary was Catholic.) There was also a different feeling to these visits, quite unlike that of necessity or chore. All the children came, as well as some other adults. One was a female friend with whom there was a sense of closeness. This same friend would stand in the cottage and talk as Mary worked in the kitchen. I remember that she talked a lot. At some point in time the name Molly, or something similar, seemed to be attached to the memory of this friend.

When I myself was young I used to dress up on Sundays. When asked why, I would say, quite simply, 'Because it's Sunday.' I didn't understand why that might seem an inadequate explanation. It seemed to make perfect sense to me, even though my family were not churchgoers.

It took me years to realise and accept that Mary's husband was also present on these trips to church. The memory of him was like a kaleidoscope, shifting from one vague picture to another. He seemed to be a taciturn man, seldom around, although there were flashes of a younger and happier person, someone who was very important to Mary. Mostly he seemed peripheral — almost as thought I was trying to block out memories of him.

A lot of the remembering was in isolated fragments, and sometimes I would have difficulty making sense of them. But other parts were complete and very detailed. It was something like a jigsaw with certain pieces faded and others temporarily mislaid, but enough of them present and clear to give a fair overall whole. The children occupied a large part

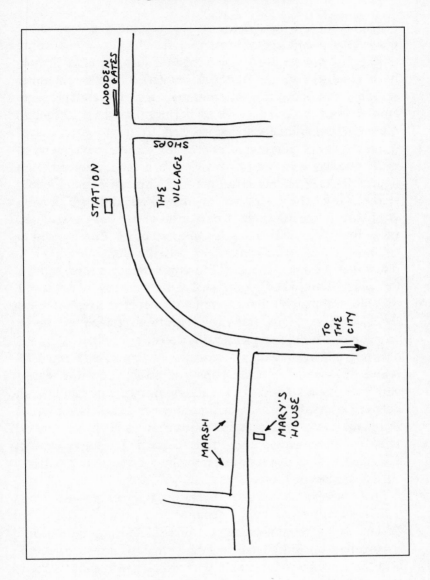

A map of the village where Mary lived, first drawn in childhood from dreams and memories.

7

of the memories, as did the cottage and its position. Other places and people seemed less precise.

There was a smallish black dog, for instance, but it must have belonged to the children because I don't remember walking it. There were other animals near the cottage, farm animals, but I was not able to be more specific. I seem to remember an animal trapped, as well.

There was a worry about shopping. There never seemed to be enough money to buy very much food, and although vegetables may have been grown in the patch I remembered at the side of the cottage, I felt that either the patch or the vegetables were in some sense borrowed. I also associated shopping with market stalls running down one side of a cobbled street which ended in a letterbox on the corner. I remember walking from the end where the letterbox was on my right. This was also the side where the stalls were, and they stood almost all the way along the cobbled street. Behind the stalls were shops, but they were much too expensive to buy goods from and so were barely considered. The stalls sold a variety of goods, mainly foodstuffs – vegetables, fresh fish, sometimes meat. There were some stalls with clothing which may have been second-hand, and one or two with household items. The whole scene was one of bustle, and the point of being there was to try to find a bargain. I don't remember actually buying very much. The confusing thing was that this market did not seem to be in the village, however hard I tried to place it there.

There were other pictures – smaller, fragmented memories which sometimes seemed disconnected in time so that it is difficult to be certain which part of her life they come from. I remember, as Mary, standing on a small wooden jetty for a boat to come. I was wearing a dark shawl which did not keep out the cold wind. It was dusk and there were few people about. I cannot remember who I was waiting for or when this was.

There were also thoughts about Mary's father and two older brothers, who seemed to have gone away. The relationship with her father was warm – a quiet, gentle, stocky man with a good sense of humour. He dressed untidily, in old clothes – rather scruffy probably – and I felt that some of his work involved looking after the fields. I have little memory of Mary's mother – a quiet woman who kept in the background. The feelings relating to her were less forceful, more subtle, or perhaps just vague in the same way as the memory of her was vague.

The older of the two brothers was gentle, with a deep, soft voice. The younger had a wiry build and endless energy; he was always joking and smiling. Although I was sure that they had gone away long before, they seemed very familiar and it was not until much later that I realised why. Until the age of seven, like many children, I had two imaginary friends whom nobody else seemed to be able to see or hear. These men would ask me questions and discuss ideas, they would tell me of amusing things that had happened to them, and best of all they would listen. Their characters – one only just an adult, always laughing; the other quieter and easy to communicate with – were very similar to those of Mary's brothers.

I still find it hard to see Mary herself. It was easier to see the surroundings, which is not too surprising as I see through her and the life remembered as her. I feel her personality mostly, and remember her clothes. There was a preference for blouses with sleeves that did not come down to the wrist but stopped just below the elbow and were gathered into a band. Even now, as an adult, I find myself rolling up shirt sleeves, or actually pinning and sewing up the wrist bands of blouses. Clothes for working in were dark, and I recall a long, dark wool skirt. To me, the child, it was hard to understand why my skirts felt too short to be comfortable. The image in my mind was that they should come to mid-calf, but children's skirts in the 1950s were knee-length. The fabric always felt wrong, too – much lighter than I expected.

Mary's hair was long and seemed slightly wavy; it was not heavy and curly like mine. As a child, I did not like my hair cut short; it felt wrong that way, although realistically it was easier to manage. As I grew older, I realised that Mary must have been only of average or slightly less than average height. I began to feel much too tall, for by the age of thirteen, I had reached the height of 5 foot 10 inches. I felt clumsy and ungainly, although as Mary I felt in someway neat, almost confined.

Attached to the memories of people, places and emotions were a couple of perceived certainties. I have always know that the period of time involved was from roughly 1898 to the 1930s – that this was the span of Mary's life. I also knew that her life was lived in Ireland. I can't explain why or how – the knowledge was just there in my consciousness. It caused bemusement in some ways: for instance, my brothers, who were aware of my predilection in limited ways, knew that I would only play soldiers with them if I were allowed to be an Irish soldier.

One day, as a child, I felt sure that if I could look at a map of Ireland I would know, deep down, where the village was located, and could match it with the maps I had been drawing ever since I was old enough to hold a pencil. The only map I could find was in my school atlas; with the whole of Ireland on just one page, the detail was not very great, so I would be unlikely to succeed in my hoped-for match, but I tried anyway. I sat with the map in front of me, then shut my eyes for a few moments to let memory take over. Several times I tried, and each time I was drawn back to the same spot on the map. Mary, I felt sure, must have seen maps, or I would not have been able to draw those maps of my own. The place I had been drawn to was called Malahide, and it was just north of Dublin.

2

Living with Mary

I had no cause to doubt that these memories were real. I assumed that memories of this kind were normal, and I expected everyone else to have them too.

The first time that I talked about the subject was when I was not quite four years old. I remember sitting on the tall stool in the kitchen talking with my mother. Although my family did not go to church, I had just been to Sunday school with my older brother. My mother asked me if I had enjoyed it. I had – there was a comforting feeling about the singing and the earnest discussion. But I said I couldn't understand why, if they were going to talk about life and death, they didn't mention our other lives.

On that day I discovered that reincarnation – the name for what I was experiencing – was considered to be a belief, not a fact. Furthermore, it was a belief not generally accepted in Britain. This revelation – that *my* truth was not a truth in everyone else's eyes, and that I was different – was a great shock to me, and caused me to worry and constantly question myself. I was aware that adults generally know more than children, and I did not want to be wrong.

My mother handled the situation well, although I now feel she was unsure how to react to what I was saying. She has always respected my individuality and that of my brothers, and that first time she responded carefully, not revealing any surprise. That must have helped, and her supportive and considerate attitude continued to boost me during the rest of my childhood.

It was some years later that I discovered there were yet more things that other people did not experience, which was just as much of a surprise to me. Most people, it seemed, did not have dreams about things before they happened, as I did. Again, I thought that premonition was normal, and I had no doubts because it was possible to see the result a few weeks or so after the dream. It was happening to me *now*, in this life, not far back in the past, and it could not be ignored or denied. From that point on I decided that adults were not always right, and that the views of others would not be allowed to create doubts in my mind about the things that I knew to be real.

By this time I was about eight years old. If other people were going to reject premonition which I knew to be real, then, I decided, my other feelings were probably rejected by them out of a similar lack of experience. This made me feel more secure. I had to form my own parameters of reality and accept my own normality. I would only discuss the 'unusual' things with my mother, whom I could trust. I was cautious with everyone else, even my brothers, and as a result became an introverted child.

I always felt different from other children, but could not estimate how much that was due to the past life memory. Because this was part of me, it must have been an integral part, contributing towards the whole person, and therefore not quantifiable. But I did find it hard to be a child. I could not understand the inconsequential things that other children seemed to find important. I would take things at face value and did not appreciate others' sense of humour, yet I alone would laugh at something quite different. That never changed. I was an outsider then, and remained so for my entire childhood and adolescence, never really feeling completely integrated.

However, my past life memories were not the only reason for my feeling of otherness and my sense of self-defence, of preservation of self. Things were very unhappy at home, and there was an impossible tension between my parents. We were all afraid of my father who, for various reasons, was trying to live a life into which he could not fit. Nor was he happy with his marriage. He did not mean to generate such fear, I am sure, but the situation was bad and became progressively worse. Each of us – my mother, my two brothers and myself – learned to cope by avoidance; without doubt each of us blocked out some of those years, and each was influenced detrimentally.

My paternal grandmother told us later that she found us very well-behaved and quiet children. The sad thing was that she did not realise that we were unusually so, or stop to wonder why.

This atmosphere at home may have been the over-riding factor that caused me to immerse myself in my memories of Mary, thought it is impossible to know which was greater – the fear within daily life, or the torment of the dream and dying over and over again, knowing that I was deserting the children. I once tried to change the dream as one might any ordinary nightmare, in order to escape from it. It did not work, though, because I knew that any other ending was a lie, and that I could not change something that was already history. I woke that night with worse tears and with a greater awareness of the reality of that dream in comparison with dreams that just stem from the imagination.

Perhaps because of this hiding, this existing at a different level of consciousness, the psychic element that was present in me was allowed to develop. Almost certainly the need to hang on to Mary's memories so strongly was helped by the negativity of my own childhood. Something had to fill the void created by my non-involvement with life.

I was a child with the feelings of both a child and an adult in precarious mixture inside, and this made enormous demands on my emotions. Rendered even more vulnerable by the anger and aggression endured at home, I would dream even in the classroom, so that my teachers began to label me slow or lazy. No one seemed to consider changing those labels to read highly stressed, or to investigate in a more constructive way what was happening. As a result, although I was later found to have a very high IQ, I hated school and my classmates, was bored by the predictability of lessons, and did not do well.

Probably I was considered a lonely child. I usually played alone, and the only company I regularly enjoyed was that of my two imaginary male friends. But although I did at times feel lonely, it was infinitely more comfortable to be alone than to be with too many people, as at school, or in the company of someone I did not want to spend time with. It is not generally realised that an introvert can actually be happy alone, and unhappy in a crowd.

I sometimes wonder how many people forget their past lives. The jigsaw that is my memory of Mary's life contains many pieces, of varying distinctness and clarity, and some have virtually faded away. If I had not repeatedly looked at those memory pieces and kept them clear, might they all have faded, leaving only the feelings? And what sort of feelings would be left behind – fear for the safety of all children and fear of parting from them? Or was that dream-like state of mind as much to do with the memory itself and a need to remember, as with avoidance of the present? Perhaps the two facets were inter-related, and the constant going-over of thoughts of the past may have helped lay them down in a way that the present should have been incised into my memory.

I felt I had to hold on to my memories of Mary and that small village in Ireland because they embodied purpose and need. Even quite early on I clung to a tentative wish that I might some day be able to find the cottage and begin to uncover answers to that inner torment about the children. But it was a secret wish, as only my mother knew about Mary.

I could not grow into my own life properly because there was not enough there. I had the love of my mother to keep me going, and a desire to try to protect my brothers, but there was so little else to enjoy or find meaning in. My escape into the past grew as I grew, and it was like a little death in my own life, a death of part of me that replaced part of my life.

By the age of five I had packed and tidied all my possessions, ready for a move that I knew would be inevitable – I was always very tidy, neurotically so – but it was not until I was thirteen that my parents separated. Between those ages, when not tidying and packing over and over again, keeping my possessions to a minimum, I was still dreaming. Sometimes it was about the future, sometimes about the past, but hardly ever about the present. The past had to be about Mary and Ireland; the future was about things yet to come. And when those future things came true, like my parents' long-anticipated separation, it did not strike me as unusual.

My mother, the boys and I left with virtually nothing and with nowhere to stay, except for a short time with family friends. For a while things actually got worse. We no longer had fear and repression to contend with, but now there were very real problems in trying to find somewhere to live and trying to survive. Yet, despite this, my school work began to improve and it seemed to become easier to talk to people. Never easy, perhaps, but certainly easier.

For a year or so there was little time to spend alone thinking, and Mary took a back seat in my mind. Then my mother was given a couple of rooms in a large house and a job as housekeeper. Somehow she managed to combine this with full-time adult education. Thinking back, I cannot remember seeing her eat very often while we were there.

By the time I was fifteen, my mother had managed to raise a private mortgage on a large, structurally sound, but desperately decrepit old house. After much scrubbing and cleaning we moved in, acquired a lodger and embarked at last on a life that felt worth living. The house was always full of people, and this I remember as the happiest part of my earlier life.

Once again I was able to think about Mary and Ireland, and about the children, but somehow the desperation had changed to optimism. It helped that I had become more communicative, and now felt better able to talk about things psychic, and about Mary, to people other than my mother. This was the 1960s, when almost any idea would be considered, and people were more willing to open their minds. And even if they were not, there was the chance of a good discussion. Perhaps, too, an element of 'unacceptability' is more attractive to teenagers, and so it seemed that the age of rebellion made room for me.

I needed to externalise and begin to face some of the trapped emotions, but I had not realised just how much emotion had been suppressed. All that was being released was simply the overflow. But at least it was a start, and I could verbalise my long-withheld fears about the children. I still did not fully understand *why* Mary was so frightened, but my friends' reactions, so much more positive than I had expected, gave me confidence. I began to see my memories of Mary and her children, and my tentative thoughts of proving those memories to be true, as a quest to be fulfilled.

What I did not realise at that point was just how long it would take before I would be able to travel to Ireland to find the village, and really set about finding out the truth concerning the children. We had little money, no car, and travelled hardly at all; in fact there was a familiarity about going everywhere on foot, and it did not seem to be a problem. I knew my quest was something that must be taken up later, if only for financial reasons; there was a need first to understand myself and learn how to cope with my life and all the feelings and fears involved – not only those generated by the actual memory, but also those created by my own life so far and by my own personality. For I would still drift off into my private trance world, oblivious to external activity, and was subject to mood swings. On occasion I would find myself gripped by a dark depression that would last for months at a time, with no apparent cause and no relief. This was later diagnosed as a metabolic problem that would always be with me, and may well have been inherited from my father.

My mother progressed during this time through teachers' training and into teaching, eventually following this up with Open University courses and postgraduate training. While teaching, she made a friend whose husband was a member of the St Albans Morris Dancers. The significance of this for me was that for the first time I was exposed to music close to my own innate preference. While growing up, I had only encountered the sombre tones of my father's double bass (he played in a traditional jazz band at weekends) and my mother's comprehensive taste in classical music.

At some point I borrowed a flute from one of the Morris musicians; in a week I had managed to play a couple of tunes on it, and had cut some bamboo to make a six-holed flute of my own. I was never a very good player, but at least I was able to buy a book of Irish tunes and try to work out the notes.

I do not remember exactly when I first heard Irish traditional music, but I do remember that it was like coming home. The Morris dancing music was enjoyable in a way that other music could not be, but was still not quite right. The very first time I heard the sound of the Gaelic unaccompanied voice, a door seemed to open to a different, older world which held a strange sense of mystery and beauty. I felt sure that Mary had enjoyed such music, but had no memory of when that might have been.

Time passed, and I seemed to emerge from the cocoon of semi-aware childhood into a more enjoyable young adulthood. For a while Mary was put aside in favour of the present; so much was happening. With life becoming more inviting, I took A-levels at college, not being able to cope any longer with the atmosphere of school where I felt so out of place. I was able to continue into further education, to qualify as a state-registered chiropodist.

I worked hard to gain those qualifications. Up until then life had been full of insecurity, first emotional, then financial, and I needed to create a secure future for myself. My mother had had to fight for her own financial independence and security through education later in life, and she had done so while looking after a growing family. I wanted to protect myself from any such vulnerability.

This of course would never have been possible, particularly since I had not taken into account the inevitable problems in relating properly to other people. I had become better with people in general, but my relationships with men were fraught with misunderstanding and fears beyond what most young women seem to encounter. Throughout my college years I moved from one mismatch to another, unable to understand myself, let alone the structure of a proper relationship. Some of this was undoubtedly due to my fear and the lack of affection in the relations with my father; but how much was due to the memories? I could not help thinking about all the influences that had shaped me, past present and distant past. Mary had liked her father, and that had obviously been a happy relationship, but why was it so hard to remember Mary's husband?

During those years of catastrophic affairs, the last of which deteriorated to the point where I lived in fear, I often tried to remember Mary's relationship with her husband, and whether it was a good one. Early on, he was easy to recall. A good-looking, impressive man who seemed to appear on the scene just after the First World War, he was something of an outsider – Irish, but from another area. I was sure he had been a soldier in the war. He seemed to have several jobs at first, but mainly there was something to do with large timbers and roof work, a very skilled job in which there was definite pride. A quiet man, not able to discuss feelings, he started by being the centre of Mary's life. Later he seemed to be at home less and less. He did not even seem to play a part in her thoughts for the children's future in those awful dreams of dying. Yet I felt sure that he lived on after that. I wondered whether my memories of him, if clearer, might have helped me understand my fear of close relationships, and the difficulties created by confusions that seemed to lack any basis.

Not long after I qualified I met my husband-to-be, fate having made a better choice than I had ever made alone. Before a year passed, we were home-hunting in Northamptonshire. There we came upon a small terraced cottage by open fields, in a hamlet of about a dozen houses south of a largish village. This was the only house we looked at that felt like home. I did not consciously try to follow the memory of Mary – it was much more instinctive than that – and we chose it together.

Sometimes I am asked how my husband feels about the memories. This is difficult to answer, because I cannot remember a time when he was not aware of them. He never seemed unduly worried about either the past life memories or any of the other psychic manifestations – they were just accepted as part of me. I realise that I have been very lucky.

As I learned how to be a wife – and was happy – I also learned through my job to understand people better, and became more relaxed. The incursions from Mary's life were less frequent as new experiences kept me occupied. From time to time, though, fragments of memory would emerge – some that might have been temporarily forgotten while life was so full, or some perhaps that had not previously been remembered.

Sometimes a smell or sound would be the trigger. I could see large machines surfacing the road outside the cottage in Ireland. There were children watching, and the smell of molten tar and the sound of steam engines. The Northamptonshire harvest one year created a dry, dusty smell that reminded me of sitting outside the cottage stuffing a mattress with straw and carefully closing it with small stitches. We then had to get it back through the doorway, which required help from several of the larger children (the oldest was then only about eight). It ended with everyone in fits of giggles, struggling with the over-large mattress in the limited space.

The smells of straw, sawdust and turpentine would immediately evoke thoughts of a small, roughly square room with a small window divided into a number of smaller panes. Most of the room seemed to be taken up by a large bed, or perhaps the room was so small that the bed filled too much of it. The smells seemed to be associated with the husband's work clothes. There was also a slightly musty odour of old buildings.

Another warm, dusty day brought to mind a bumpy cart trip where goods, at least two children (one still just a babe in arms) and I bounced around on the dry, uneven road. This must have been the day of moving to the cottage near Malahide. There was a sense of nervousness about the journey, and relief at having arrived. But I do not think we had travelled far. As I myself was happy, I think that the Mary memories that did come to me at that time were the happier ones.

I knew that I wanted children of my own, and I spent time preparing and making clothing for them for several years before it was necessary. Dressmaking, something that in the present I have found a fairly instinctive skill, returns frequently as a part of Mary's memory. And for some reason the youngest boy's jacket sticks in my mind, perhaps because he used to fidget with the hem as he walked. It was a wool jacket and I can remember making it by pulling apart an old coat, turning the fabric and the lining to present the unworn inner surface, and making the new jacket for the child by hand. A sense of pride in the quality of the workmanship forms part of the memory.

When my own son was born in 1979 I felt like a whole person, and there followed a few years that I will always hold dear. True to my need for security and financial independence, I did not give up work entirely; but there was also a need to be a mother, so this was given priority. In motherhood and family life, at last I began to find myself. In marriage I no longer felt alone.

Birth is a unique experience, and one that I would never want to forget. Now I was a mother myself and was able to share those feelings that had been with me for so long – the need to care for my children. This time, though, I had a real child whom I could hold close.

During those years I grew closer to understanding some of the stronger and stranger emotions relating to the memories, in particular the feelings of guilt. For mothers, guilt is a peculiarly frequent emotion. When something goes wrong, it is always taken on oneself as though everything is one's own responsibility. I could now appreciate in a much more urgent and real sense the power of Mary's emotion about leaving the children when she died. I could not even leave my son for a few hours, let alone bear the thought of total separation. I knew that I would see my children grow (I had seen some of my future); but looking at my son, the feelings of being parted from the children, as Mary, caused more thoughts to emerge. I was confident that my husband could look after his children, and was happy for him to take some of the responsibility, but I wondered if Mary did not have that same confidence. I could never quite reach in past the barriers of her sense of guilt and the intensity of her distress, but something felt very uncomfortable.

Soon we were to be hit by an economic crisis that forced me to work longer hours, although still very much part-time. During this period in 1983, my second child was born. She was planned when things were bad, but by the time she was born things had got much worse. My husband was by now self-employed, in a period when businesses everywhere were failing. He was in haulage: overheads were becoming crippling, and profits were fast disappearing. Our security was shattered. I took very little time off before my daughter was born and only three weeks afterwards. I too was working on a self-employed basis, and had to work so that we could eat.

The obsession with the past, although less to the forefront, was never forgotten. It lay in wait for the right time, and re-emerged slowly. As my children grew and the strength of my maternal feeling was nurtured by their love, so the need grew to find that other family. Those children had been deprived at an early age of what my own children were now enjoying, and I felt that I had to do something about it. It seemed no coincidence that the need to search intensified as I grew nearer to the age that Mary was when she died – her early thirties. And neither perhaps was it a coincidence that this was also, simultaneously, the beginning of one of the most stressful phases of my life. For it had not occurred to me that, through seeking and facing the past, I would also unearth my own inadequacies and have to face myself as well.

Throughout the years I had been making notes about the memories, speaking to people about Mary, and sharing my feelings. I had also been – in a fairly haphazard way, I must admit – seeking out maps of Ireland, to see if I could find one which would give a clearer picture of Malahide, the village I believed to be Mary's home, and which would correspond to the maps I had drawn in childhood.

In 1980 a new bookshop, the Towcester Bookshop, opened near our home, and one day I ordered from them a map at the scale of a quarter inch to the mile which covered the Malahide area. I knew it could not be very detailed, but it would be better than the school atlas and everything else that I had seen so far. I told the owner of the shop, Mr Peter Gooding, why I wanted the map and showed him my hand-drawn versions. If he felt that I was just a little odd, he did not give it away.

When the map arrived Mr Gooding telephoned me, and I took my own map with me to the shop for comparison. All the roads that I had marked appeared on the new map. I had placed the roads and landmarks so that north was correctly positioned at the top, and the distances between the roads were fairly well to scale. The station was where I had marked it, and the road that I had marked 'To the

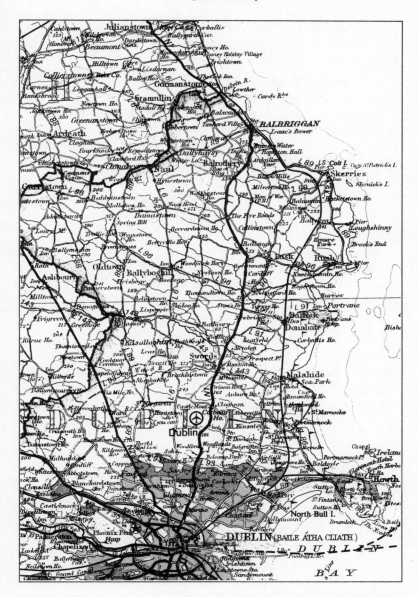

A section of the map ordered from the Towcester Bookshop in 1980.
(© Bartholomew. Reproduced with permission.)

City' was the Dublin road. What Mr Gooding and I had witnessed together was strong evidence that all along I had been drawing a fairly accurate map of Malahide. This was my first confirmation that the dreams and memories were real, and not just a product of my imagination. This was exactly the spur I needed to begin my search for Mary's life, and for the children she had left behind.

3

First Steps into My Past

Having made my decision, I realised I had very little to go on. All I had was a collection of mind 'snapshots' of a young Irishwoman, her family and children, her home and her death. I had identified where I thought she had lived in Ireland, and that, I believed, had been proved by the new map. And where should I begin? I did not even have a surname for Mary and her family. That was no surprise to me, since I have always been bad at names. I once forgot my own brother's name when introducing him to someone else, and if Mary's surname had cropped up in the memories or dreams, it would have been quite in character for me to have forgotten it. However, without that name I did not see how anything positive could be done at such a distance. If I had had some money I would have visited Malahide in person, but we were struggling as it was, and such expenditure was impossible.

I talked about it all endlessly with my husband, my mother and close friends, and their support was invaluable. They didn't react over-much, but the very fact that they would

draw my attention to anything psychic or past life stories –
'I heard something the other day that might interest you' –
was in itself confirmation of acceptance. Even when talking
to people whom I did not know very well I found a strong
interest in both psychic matters and reincarnation. Many
would see it as a chance to unload something in their own
lives that had mystified them, something they would not
normally have discussed for fear of ridicule or disbelief –
the very emotions that had repressed me for so long.

I had many discussions, too, with a local vicar, who was
quite able to accept that there was more in the world than
just the obvious or ordinary. Once I had begun to air my
feelings on things psychic, the subject was guaranteed to
arise on every occasion that we met. He too had a number
of stories of unexplained happenings that he was enthusiastic
to explore in an open and unbiased way.

I also met people who shared my psychic abilities. I
enrolled in an evening class in one of the martial arts –
in which there is an understanding of spirit and *chi*, the
inner energy – and after one class I mentioned my psychic
interests to the instructor. Looking at him, I realised that he
too had, and could use, psychic ability. First I asked him
for something of his that I could hold; this was intended
to demonstrate psychometry, in order to define what I was
trying to explain. He gave me his van keys but without
saying what they were. I described the inside of his van
and when I said that, down to my left, near the handbrake,
there was bare metal where there should have been carpet,
he became very excited. Everything I had described was
completely accurate. At this point I explained that it was not
such an unusual ability; I gave him my ring, and projected
thought to encourage a response. He felt heat from the ring,
and was able to describe feelings that were mine, feelings
sufficiently alien to him to convince him that this was a
very real phenomenon.

One of the people outside my immediate family whom I felt most able to discuss things with was Mr Coulter, a retired gentleman, originally from southern Ireland, who was very widely read. It was whilst talking to him that the subject of reincarnation was first seriously brought up as a possible explanation for my memories. Firstly, in the interests of investigating every avenue, he wondered if there were some sort of genetic relationship with Mary's family. I knew I had an Irish great-grandmother, but she was west coast Irish, with no Dublin connections; she had lived in Malta and India in her earlier years, and so far as I knew never even saw Ireland. The other side of the family had been traced back to the Domesday Book, so there was complete documentation there. Some kind of genetic telepathy was certainly not the answer in this particular case.

Eventually it was the *strength* of the emotions and the memories that I experienced as Mary that convinced us that her life had been real, and that I was reliving a past life through reincarnation. No child could possibly have invented what I experienced, and relating discussions with my mother convinced Mr Coulter that the memories had actually been part of me throughout my entire life.

Reincarnation is probably the most ancient belief of all, despite the fact that three of the major religions – Christianity, Judaism and, to a lesser extent, Islam – deny it. Basically, the adherents of reincarnation believe that all humans possess an eternal, non-physical element or energy which will not die when the physical body dies, but will leave that body and enter another some time later, and do so again and again.

This is fairly consistent with scientific thought. It is stated as a law of physics that energy cannot be either created or destroyed, but can only be changed. Reincarnation would allow this energy to be preserved. It also allies with the Christian idea of the immortality of the soul. If the soul *is* immortal, then logically it can have no beginning and no end. There would seem to be a continuum, or continuity, with a survival of the soul throughout many lifetimes and many bodies, perhaps even through thousands of years. I myself had vague memories of other times, which were perhaps other lives, although all were very much less clear than Mary.

Mr Coulter and I discussed many other aspects of reincarnation and books written on the subject. One of the most interesting books was *Children Who Remember Previous Lives* (University Press of Virginia) by Dr Ian Stevenson, who had studied children, many of them from Asia (where of course reincarnation is much more accepted than in the West). A number of these children had spontaneous and incredibly detailed memories of fairly recent previous lives. The majority remembered lives that had been ended before their logical time – by violence or illness – and Dr Stevenson offered the explanation that the 'souls' may have felt incomplete, that there was a sense of life unfinished, thus the fairly swift reincarnation. (Dr Stevenson's research was also aided by this 'speed', as many of the relatives of the people whose lives had ended were still available to be interviewed.)

To me this sense of unfinished business rang true as a possible explanation of the urgency of Mary's memories, their remarkable consistency, and the tenacity with which they had remained in my consciousness throughout the whole of my life. Responsibility for one's children was, I now knew at first hand, the primary emotion of a mother, and Mary's guilt at leaving them did imbue my being and my emotions with a strong sense of a task unfinished and incomplete. That there was a sense of *fear* there as well was less easy to comprehend. However, for Mary's sake, if not for my own, I would have to take the investigation further and find her children.

By some coincidence, just when I was beginning to feel that my experiences were not too abnormal, I became involved in a small scientific study. The martial arts instructor's wife had talked to a teacher who was in the process of upgrading her qualifications by taking a degree course. The teacher had asked if she knew of anyone who was psychic, as she was looking for volunteers for an experiment she wished to conduct as part of her thesis.

When the teacher and I made contact I told her of the wooden beam that we had placed as an upright to finish the edge of a removed wall. The timber had been reclaimed, and when I first touched it I felt that I was high in the roof of a barn. As I explained this, I was touching the timber to show her, and before I had finished the story the teacher also described the feeling of the timber being from a barn. We both felt that psychometric experience simultaneously.

As she wanted to carry out a test of psychic ability on each subject before he or she was included in the experiment, this was of value. Each subject was then to be tested individually for psychic activity whilst connected to an electroencephalograph, a device used by doctors and psychologists to record electrical activity within the brain. Electrodes sense these electrical impulses, or brain waves, and convert them into signals which are recorded as lines on a moving strip of paper. An ordinary ECG trace has a few squiggles in the lines; heightened brain activity is recorded by violent peaks and troughs in the lines, rather like those created by an earthquake on a seismograph.

At Nene College, Northampton, the electrodes were attached to my head with the resinous adhesive needed to conduct electrical current. For the psychic part of the test I again used psychometry – holding an item belonging to a person, then visualising and describing images related to that person, such as surroundings familiar to them, and sometimes feelings of some predominant emotion.

When I concentrated on the object – a watch belonging to the technician – the graph recorded an extremely intense level of brain activity, much higher than during the first, ordinary part of the test. After a few minutes of talking, the technician took the watch back and stopped the experiment. The details I was giving about her thoughts on her home and her work had begun to make her feel emotionally exposed. She agreed with what I had revealed, though. This was obviously of great help in my teacher friend's field of research, but for me it was yet another step towards a more general acceptance of my experiences.

Meeting the teacher had an important spin-off, because through her I was introduced to a man whose hobby was hypnotic regression. He was researching the actual phenomenon of previous lives, not operating as a therapist. He would hypnotise his subjects, then tell them to go back in time, either to earlier stages in their own present lives or to a possible former life or lives.

In late 1987 the hypnotist was going to give a talk and demonstration at a school in Northampton, and the teacher suggested I went. At that time I was recovering from one of my periodic depressions – they seemed to return about every eighteen months – and I did not really want to face crowds of people. But, perhaps because of that relentless inner drive to find out more about my experiences, I went after all.

During the lecture, which he gave to an audience of about sixty people, individual and group hypnosis was used. Time was allotted for questions, and I felt I had to ask whether the hypnotist had come across anyone like me before. He already knew of me, and I was asked to go to the front, which was quite nerve-racking.

We discussed my memories and the dream, and then he asked if I was prepared to be hypnotised there and then; but I was far too self-conscious and afraid of the experience itself to agree.

However, the second time I met the hypnotist, at a meeting in somebody's house quite close to home, I allowed myself to be hypnotised in front of about a dozen people – members of a women's group. This was on 6 January 1988. Under hypnosis I described the cobbled street with market stalls down one side, and Mary's last moments. I knew this scene well. Many times as a child I had woken from that dream, knowing the anguish of a woman destined to die before her children had grown. I cried as she cried; I knew her pain as my own. I did not want to leave, but knew that I would and that I could do nothing to prevent it. There was fear for the children and worry over how they would manage. The anger and unfairness outweighed any pain that death might bring. This memory was the one that I had never been able to escape from, the one that usually came to me when I was alone at night.

Going through Mary's death again in this way, I found tears rolling down my face in a quite uncontrollable manner. Normally I would not allow myself to be seen crying in public, but the hypnosis took me to a level of mind where I seemed unable to apply normal constraints.

After this session I was offered a course of hypnotic regression, due to start on 10 February, that would be documented and tape-recorded. There was no fee involved, as it was a hobby. I accepted; this was what I needed. I felt I could substantiate many of the memories, even perhaps learn more about Mary, her life and her children. I might even end up with a clearer picture of the names, particularly that elusive surname, without which I thought I could not proceed in my search.

*

Hypnotic regression began with a French psychoanalyst and hypnotherapist, Colonel Albert de Roches, who in 1903 wrote a book in which he claimed to have regressed people through their childhoods, through pre-natal memory and even further back through past lives. (He also claimed to have patients who had given accounts of future lives. My own experience shows that this type of awareness is also possible without hypnosis.) People were very skeptical of his claims, then and afterwards, until the famous 1950s' American case of Bridie Murphy, the past life regression of Virginia Tighe, by amateur hypnotist Morey Bernstein. After that, other hypnotists began to find that patients were regressing, often accidentally, and interest in the subject grew.

Although hypnotic regression has become so popular, it is apparently not highly valued by serious researchers, as the information given by an adult under hypnosis can have come from a variety of sources. However, for me this was a new experience, and the object was not so much to try to search for past life memories but to add anything of use to a memory that was verifiably detailed from early childhood. I wanted to utilise all possible means to find sufficient detail to be certain that, if a family were found, I could be quite sure that it was *my* family.

Hypnosis is a strange experience even without the element of regression. All sorts of memories which have been hidden deep within the subconscious and cannot ordinarily be reached can be brought to the surface. This is double-edged – both a wonderful and a disturbing experience at the same time. Some of the memories that people push into the deep recesses of their minds are there for a good reason – perhaps because these are the memories they are unable or unwilling to face, and which have been hidden for self-protection. By lifting and exposing any deep memory, one is forced to look again at both the forgotten and the repressed.

I was the first person the hypnotist had worked with who had a past life memory already, prior to hypnosis. A room had been commandeered to allow space for recording equipment, record files and a large, comfortable chair where I might relax sufficiently to allow such intrusion into my mind as was necessary. I knew this would feel somewhat invasive, but my need to find out was great enough to suppress my instinct for privacy. Cooperation was, I felt, the only way to unlock the doors and release more details that might help me trace Mary's family.

I sat uneasily in the over-large chair, almost as nervous as I had been on that first occasion. He asked me if he had left a trigger, a subconscious command that would help him put me under more quickly. I told him that he had, but I was not sure whether, after a month, it would still work. The trigger was a touch on my shoulder, and it worked so fast that I hardly managed to finish my sentence before slipping into that strange slumber. There was a sensation of falling, followed by fighting, resisting a little, then at last sinking into a vast and deep chasm of semi-consciousness.

First of all he asked me to remember a time in my own past. Luckily it was early childhood he asked me to recall, so the memories were not too uncomfortable. I had to describe my first school and the person I sat next to on the bus. Then, stage by stage, I was taken further back until he asked me to return to a time before I was born and to talk about what I discovered there.

I found myself recognisably as Mary, but it was not in the cottage and it was before the children were born. This was a young Mary, before marriage, something I had not consciously remembered before. He asked questions and I was aware of listening to them, but I also listened to the answers, and it seemed to take a little while before I realised that it was my own voice answering. It was as though I were a spectator, existing partly in that place I could see, and partly in the present.

Yet I was Mary, and the past had become very real. I could smell the grass on the slopes outside a large farmhouse, and I breathed in the fresh spring air. I felt that this was where I worked for the Lett family. The farmhouse was near a small village, but here I was in open fields. The hypnotist asked me how I was dressed. Although I knew he was asking Mary the questions, it seemed that it was my other self who answered, because now I was Mary and too involved with what was going on to answer. Looking down at my clothes, I heard my dissociated voice answering: 'A long dark wool skirt and an apron. The apron is not so long but the skirt nearly reaches the ground.'

At the farmhouse, feeling that this was a place I knew, I saw Mary cleaning the grate and laying a fire. I saw a number of rooms in the house. This was not the memory I had expected to see. I was so used to seeing the cottage at Malahide that I had assumed that this was where I would find myself.

Someone said: '1915'. I realised that it was my voice, so the hypnotist must have asked the year and she had answered. I was drifting between the two personalities. He also asked for an age; there was some hesitation and then: 'Seventeen'.

I walked briskly down the hill from the house to the village. The place was to the north of Dublin but was not Malahide, yet I felt that it was not far from there. In the village was the house where my family lived. There was a small stone house standing on its own, and thoughts of Mary's father came to me, and of her brothers. The hypnotist asked for names, but all I could give was a street called something like 'Walldown Lane'. I also saw a smithy and a shop that was in someone's house front. I was asked to describe it, and say what sort of things it sold. My mind focused on ribbons, and on the fact that apparently it often ran out of bread.

As the questions were being asked and answered in this strange, mechanical way, I seemed to be free to wander through the places I saw – tangible, vivid places. I felt the wind in my hair; I could touch and smell the air as though I were there.

He asked to see 1919. Mary was walking down a main street. Behind me, a tall brick wall swept round to a pair of wooden gates. On the corner of the street was a letterbox, and the ground was uneven. He asked what I was wearing and I described a hand-made calf-length skirt with an overlaid scalloped border, the underlayer being in a contrasting fabric. I felt pride in the needlework.

Beside Mary was her husband, a smartly dressed man of perhaps twenty-five. At this time he was the centre of Mary's attention; there were no children yet. He seemed a little distant, perhaps arrogant, and as Mary looked at him, he turned around to see if he was being noticed by anyone else.

Time drifted and I was asked to describe what I could see, which I realised was Malahide. I was in the main north-to-south road in the middle of the village, and mentioned a butcher's shop on the west side about two or three buildings down from the north end.

I was asked about the husband. Pressed for a name, I eventually and reluctantly said: 'Bryan', a name I had used in childhood games. I was uncertain, though, if it was the right one here. I was asked what he did for a job, and described the large timbers up high and some other jobs before he went back – but back where? I did not know. There were queries that related to the First World War, but although I had always thought of him as a soldier, my response seemed clouded and confused. Perhaps I was trying too hard to give the right answers.

Later I was being asked about a church which I knew to be on the same road and on the same side as the butcher's shop, but quite a way further down. There was a large gable end close to the road, with coping stones along the top and piers at each side with a stone on top. In front was a wooden notice-board with some engraving around it. This gable end was the main view of the church. The outside was easy to describe but the inside was not, suggesting a building passed regularly but not necessarily entered. I felt that this church was not Catholic, but as I had always assumed Mary to be Catholic there was some confusion. There seemed no immediate reason for this church to be relevant.

I was asked about weddings, and saw one in this particular church. It could have been a friend's wedding, though I had been asked about my own. Or Mary could have been acting as a paid witness, then a fairly common way of earning a little extra money. There seemed so few people that this was a distinct possibility. Other scenes that may well have been from Mary's wedding were infused into the picture, so that there was a confusion of times and events, and I felt it was of little real value. I was also instructed to look in the register and give a name and date, which were offered with unlikely clarity. The name given was O'Neil, and the date was 1921. I was not at all sure that these were correct.

Later I saw Mary's home, the one I usually remember. It was a fairly traditional cottage, the first on the left along the straight, dusty lane running west from the south end of Malahide, and was something less than a mile from where the lane began. Other details seemed to be consistent with my previous dreams and memories.

I was taken further forwards in time and described a small girl running at my feet. She had a mop of darkish hair with perhaps a touch of red as the sunlight caught it. I gave her date of birth as 4 February 1922, and although this seemed less confused than the church and wedding, once more I found myself questioning the precision of the answer. The rough date felt right, but the exactness I doubted.

Too soon I was being woken, taken away from what I was trying to understand and remember. Slowly I awoke, trying to move, but at first my limbs failed to respond, as though paralysed. After a few moments full consciousness returned, as did mobility. What had felt like only ten minutes, a glance at the clock assured me, was an hour.

When I got home later that evening I made rapid notes, hoping that there might be just one piece of useful information. The names O'Neil and Bryan didn't seem quite right, but I had ventured further back into Mary's life than ever before and seen many new things. I marked the positions of the butcher's shop and the church on one of my maps so that they might one day be checked. I even noted the dates about which I was so dubious. I desperately needed to find a key to start my search, and anything might turn out to be that key. I felt as thought I had taken the first step towards completing a quest I had waited half a lifetime to fulfil.

Two weeks later I went back for my second visit to the hypnotist. This time he was interested in looking at the time between the 1930s, when Mary died, and my own birth in 1953. This was more relevant to his own research into the phenomenon of past lives than to my search for Mary's family, although I was interested. It could even be useful in understanding or proving continuity of the 'soul' which is one of the major concepts in most reincarnation theories.

This time, when I was touched on the shoulder, I was instructed to go to the last memories of Mary. Once again I was forced to endure the physical pain and anguish that, in some perverse way, I almost needed to experience, as though the very familiarity would refuel my determination. Slowly moving through the pain to the point where only emotions remained, I began to enter that other state.

It was in the autumn when Mary died. She looked thin as my viewpoint drifted to some point above and a little to one side of her now vacant body. The room was white and empty. I had died alone in what looked like a hospital. Time seemed irrelevant, so I could not say how much later Mary's husband entered the room. He sat by the bed, hunched over it. For the first time I was aware of his feelings. He seemed less able at that moment to hide his emotions behind indifference or off-handedness. Too late, I had some insight into the man he could have been if he had been more able to express his feelings. I was no longer close, but had continued to drift further away into a very calm darkness. Time itself ceased to be definable; everything felt dampened as though in suspended animation or hibernation.

Somewhere in the blackness, as I was talked through the years by the voice of the hypnotist, was a small memory. In 1940 it was still black, but there was a subtle change of awareness that I can only describe as a need to 'be something' again. By 1945 there was a small child. Nothing was very clear this time, but there was a feeling of being alone or just lonely. There was noise, confusion and untidiness.

The hypnotist, that almost forgotten controller of this excursion into another realm, drew me away, back in time again to Ireland. I saw a growing family, and there was a little impatience as Mary found herself less entranced with the joys of parenthood now that there was a houseful of children. Briefly I described several of the children consistently with previous memory, and mentioned a baby boy who died at birth. It was a brief look, and I was unable to gain more than a vague impression.

I heard the voice directing me again to drift further back, a long way back − several hundred years. By chance I found myself in one of the memories that had been with me since childhood, although I did not at first recognise it as such. Of the several memories, Mary has always been the strongest and the most detailed.

I seemed to stop, suddenly petrified. For several minutes I described the fears of a seven-year-old French country girl – Anna, I think – who had been sold into service to a household in Boulogne. Pictures of a large family and a farmhouse left behind. A trip with her father and the fear of never seeing her family again. Many details, the year 1716. As if the trauma of Mary's memories was not enough, this terror was now left in my conscious mind. Familiar feelings of injustice and anger mingled with fear, all having tangibility in this other time and place.

Too soon the voice drew me back to the present, and I was left with shreds of memory, some tantalising, some terrifying. . . .

I began to feel that this experience of regression through hypnosis was consuming my thoughts. Doors left slightly ajar were now opening up so wide, and at such a speed, that there was little time to come to terms with the significance of what was going on. I was finding the detail overwhelming, and tried to cope with it by questioning the accuracy either too much or not enough.

It irritated me that with hypnosis it was so easy to gain a level of recall and of detail that I was unable to reach by myself, even after years of practice. I was annoyed that it had taken so long to find out that this was possible, and wondered if I had wasted all those years. Time became my enemy. I wanted to know everything and find my family *now*. The two weeks between each session began to hurt. It was like an addiction, and I did not want it to stop until I had all the answers I wanted. It never occurred to me that I might need this time and some more maturity before I was ready to go forward. It was just too difficult to accept that patience was needed for those first steps.

However, the feeling of opening a Pandora's box remained. Up until then I had locked away in a less prominent part of my consciousness my frustration at not being able to do anything about finding the children and my overwhelming anger about the situation. I had had to do this in order to function in normal life. The hypnosis, however, was breaking down all those barriers that I had erected to protect myself from part of the pain. Although I could always remember and always *feel* the pain, I had rationalised everything to enable me to carry on as myself. The intensity of remembering under hypnosis left me feeling opened up, raw, vulnerable and confused. There was a tremendous conflict between self-preservation and the needs from the past. From a psychological point of view it is often better to face things than repress them, but the trauma of doing so should not be underestimated.

At the next session, guided straight back to Mary, I spoke without being asked. 'My baby is dead.' The hypnotist asked questions which seemed to be answered almost mechanically, but I was involved with the past. I could see a woman – a nurse, I assumed. She handed me the dead baby so that I could hold it and say goodbye.

The grief at the loss was present at that time, in this time, and is present still, each time the memory is brought to mind. I held the baby and understood. I felt thankful that it was possible to say goodbye like this, to look on the child destined not to live. Much easier than to be told, but not allowed to see or say goodbye. Had there been another time when Mary had not said goodbye? Perhaps. The feeling of this being a better way was strong. There was no sense of frustration or injustice – just grief, a sense of loss released at the time of loss, normal feelings easy to accept now.

It was a boy. Mary had several boys, and was now in her thirties. I was asked if it was a good age to have children, and replied that it was not unusual. But inside there was anger at the question – a stupid question. As if there were any choice about having children. Whose thoughts, I wondered, am I now thinking?

He took me back again. My mind obediently responded to the direction and I found myself sitting on a grassy slope. Before me was a panoramic view of rolling hills running down to water far off in the distance. Not fresh water, I think, but an inlet perhaps, as there seemed to be land beyond the water; or perhaps this was the sea and before me was an island. I the observer did not know, and I the person past did not worry. I could smell the earth and moist plants. I wanted to be able to get up and walk out over the hills for miles, so beautiful was the landscape.

The hypnotist was talking about work, asking questions. Mary did not want to think about work while sitting here. How old? Fifteen. To be stuck in that big house cleaning all day. No, it was much better to be out here than to think about work. This young Mary was more slight in build than later, and perhaps a little unrealistic in outlook yet. But she had the same optimism and cheerfulness that were to help later.

Mary liked Mrs Lett. The hypnotist was asking me all sorts of things about her and the house. There were white pillars on either side of the porch, but it was not a mansion, just a big farmhouse. Mrs Lett would sit in the main room which occupied the full depth of the right side of the house and had windows front and back. She was fairly old and did not go out much. The main room was wonderful, with a large carpet rich with colours, warm reds and russets, filling most of the floor. On the walls were framed mirrors and about the room stood chairs with arms and lots of other beautiful furniture. Desks and tables, nothing large, everything elegant – even Mrs Lett with her pearl necklace and pale face. There were things here that were obviously beyond Mary's usual experience, a level of wealth that she had not been able to see close to until working here.

He let me move through the house and describe what I could see. There were several floors. On the first floor was a long landing with about three or four doors leading to rooms. The second-floor rooms were made small by the angle of the roof, and were used mainly for storage.

There were other people – someone in the kitchen, a cook probably. The kitchen was at the back left side of the house where there were also a small washroom and utility rooms. The cook did not do the tiresome or dirty jobs. Mary cleaned and scrubbed and washed. The cold outer room where these jobs were done was only glimpsed briefly – there was no magic there, no reason to linger or look; it was just a place to be when there was work to be done.

The hypnotist asked me to go forward in time a little. Now Mary was married with a family, and cleaning the cottage. He asked me about household tasks and what I was using to clean with. Part of me understood why he asked these questions, but another part of me was of that time and did not understand. The replies were sometimes curt: 'A damp cloth.' All the surfaces were wiped clean with a cloth. He asked me about washing clothes. I could see a block of soap which was used to scrub the clothes before washing them. He then asked me about dishes. The level of irritation was rising as I described soap in small flakes that was used for dish-washing, whilst knowing full well that there was none in the house: it cost too much.

It was quiet – most of the children were at school. He asked about the school, but I was unable to see a name: just the letter C. I did not know if they used slates, but had seen a book that the eldest girl had written in. She was bright and did well at school. I had great hopes for her. She was clever, patient and hard-working enough to achieve higher things – becoming a nurse, perhaps. One of the older boys – not the eldest, though – was difficult at times, and over-energetic. I described the other children much as I had described them before.

Again the instruction came to go some other place in time, back to France and Anna in Boulogne. Then forward again beyond Mary and, step by step, to the child between 1940 and 1945. Much detail, names, a street name in Hendon, London (which was later found to exist). A short memory of a short life.

Then I was taken forward again, through the darkness, slowly, until there was a light ahead which at first was just a spot. I wanted to go towards it. As I reached it there was a feeling of warmth, actual physical warmth and comfort, and this occurred after a time of no physical awareness. There was now a sense without other senses, a sense of *being*.

As an observer, I found this hard to accept, yet at the time I did seem to understand what it was about. My conscious self knew that we had reached a point before my own birth, and that what was happening related to pre-birth memory.

Awareness and senses grew; then there was a confined security as though I was held tightly, followed by light and noise and people. My head emerged facing left and then turned upwards. There was no security now, just noise and confusion, then fairly soon the need to be held as closely confined as before, for comfort and security. Soon that need was being fulfilled, but too briefly; very quickly, it seemed, I was being taken away and did not want to go. I was not being held firmly, and I was neither secure and close, nor where I had wanted to stay.

This was all observed with amazement and some incredulity, but the hypnotist spoke again and lifted me from that time, drawing my mind back to the present. He tried to calm the anxiety that remained, speaking of a positive attitude and saying that unfinished tasks from the past should be left. I began to think that such thoughts on his part were counter to my own direction. I had a lifetime's habit of not leaving the past – or at least, truer to say, *it* would not leave *me*, nor could it. Perhaps he had become aware at last of the sense of guilt that Mary's death caused me, or perhaps he thought it unlikely that I would be able to find the family or any peace. He may even have thought it was the unrest and insecurity of my entry into this life that prompted the concern.

I checked later with my mother about the position of my head during birth and about being taken away, and found that I had 'seen' the whole thing fairly accurately. She especially remembered my head turning up, as she could see my face. As to being taken away, it was the midwife's first delivery and she was so delighted that I was such a large and mature-looking baby that she took me all round the hospital to show to everyone before I was given back to my mother. I wonder if this has anything to do with my aversion to crowds of people and noise, and being in the limelight?

Research has proved that, under hypnosis, people can remember the position of their head at birth. Every person in the experiment I read about had accurately described their own birth position to a researcher who was not allowed access to the birth records until after the hypnosis questioning. But pre-birth memory is less easy to prove.

The project began to affect my daily life, but as it was never out of my mind this should not have been surprising. The depth of emotion entwined within the surfacing visions of the past was extreme and at times unbearable. Memories were also rising up between hypnotic sessions and adding to the information that needed to be assessed and understood.

I became immensely frustrated, primarily because every-thing seemed to be moving at too leisurely a pace. The hypnotist himself was slow and methodical, probably a prerequisite of the task. I felt like a child waiting for Christmas, but having no understanding of the period of time the waiting involved.

On my next visit to the hypnotist, he was still interested in looking at many different times. Our first excursion was to a place a thousand years ago – Wales in the Dark Ages. A few details emerged, such as the mode of dress and woven fabric used, that turned out later to be historically correct. This took a bit of research but it boosted my growing confidence that there was accuracy in the things I had seen.

He took me back to find Mary, but there was so much jumping backwards and forwards in time that it was hard to remember it all. The intention was to check dates, names and events for continuity. I did remember a telephone number that was given as that for the Lett's house – 71 34 with some figures in front, perhaps 61 or 6 something. That was useful, as it could be checked. (Later I discovered that Irish telephone numbers are made up of six digits in three pairs – as I had given them – and the number given would be viable for the area where I expected the farmhouse to be, near Dublin.)

I saw a doctor who visited Mrs Lett, partly as a friend. He wore a long dark coat and a hat with a dent in the crown. He drove about the only car I had seen; it was black and shiny, with huge wheel arches.

There were books in the main room, in a bookcase towards the back of the house against an inside wall. The hypnotist asked me about their titles, but I did not answer. I could see one by Tolstoy and other classics, but my present self was unable to accept that such detail could be accurate. Confused, I said too little, yet I could see the whole room in perfect detail.

The farmhouse itself was set high on a hill with extensive views, especially to the back, in, I think, a south-west direction. I also seem to remember an interest in someone up on a roof, on one of the outbuildings – might this have been the young man who became Mary's husband?

This was a less satisfactory session. Although it was fascinating to look back through other times and places, some familiar and some not, I wondered about the relevance. These memories achieved little towards my own quest.

By now my enthusiasm was running without check, like a train without a driver. I felt unable to control the extremes of emotion bubbling up through my subconscious and taking over so much of my time. The fact that I still had insufficient information, and that it possibly was not yet right to forge ahead, was not a consideration.

I was given an extra impetus by a gift from Mr Coulter. I had been talking obsessively to him and other friends in between all these hypnosis sessions, and bemoaning the lack of verifiable detail in so many areas. After one of his trips to Ireland he brought me back an Ordnance Survey map of the Dublin area, at one inch to the mile. This was very much more detailed than the maps I had already consulted, and I could hardly contain my excitement. Not only were the station and churches marked where I had placed them, either originally or later after the hypnosis, but the road conformations were even more clearly those that I had drawn as a child. Names suddenly leaped at me – 'Gay Brook' (more usually spelt as one word) in particular – but, most exciting of all, I saw the line of the stream that I had always known was near to Mary's cottage.

Now I felt a great need to check more of the details, and I began to wonder how I could do. I decided to contact someone of the surname I had given under hypnosis, trusting, perhaps foolishly, that it was more accurate than I had thought. The impatience caused by waiting more than thirty years before being able to do something definite about finding Mary's family affected any natural caution. Although I felt it was

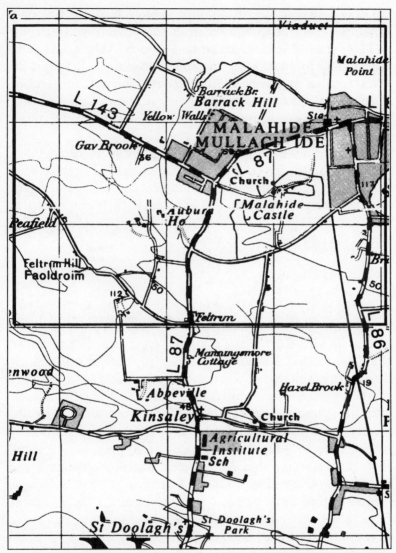

The Ordnance Survey map brought back in 1988 by Mr Coulter. A good comparison can be made between the boxed section and the maps I drew in childhood. (Based on the Ordnance Survey by permission of the Government. Permit No. 5746.)

inevitable that some of the details would be correct – so much matched the existing memories – I knew it was wildly unlikely I would find anyone this way. But there had to be something to hold on to, something to do.

So I went to the local library and got out the Dublin telephone book; under 'O'Neil' I noted down several who lived with in a reasonable radius of Malahide. I chose one, and sent him a letter.

Dear Mr O'Neil,

Please excuse the intrusion but I am trying to trace a family who lived fairly near to you. They may have had the same family name, and I wondered if there was any family connection.

The family I am searching for lived in the first cottage on the left on the road marked on the map enclosed. This was during the 1920s and 1930s. There were at least six or more children, and the mother, whose name I believe was Mary, died in the 1930s.

Yours sincerely,
Jenny Cockell

With the letter went a copy of the street map I had drawn, now with the identifying names of Malahide, Swords and Gaybrook. I made the enquiry sound as if it were simply a genealogical one, thinking that it would be unreasonable to expect a reply if the real reason were given; most people would find that too odd to cope with.

This first letter represented an explosion of all my pent-up frustration and emotional need. I had tried to be patient and wait until the hypnotist was ready, but somewhere out there was the answer, and no longer could I apply constraints

50

to that urgent, desperate, passionate need. This letter was my first real step towards accepting the phenomenon on a real-life basis, and brought the memories one step further out of repression, one step further into the daylight.

4

Need for Proof

The thought foremost in my mind at this time was to find the family and discover how the children managed after the death of their mother. Long shots like the letter helped towards that end. Not long afterward I sent off similar letters to other O'Neils in the area, and I waited with eager anticipation for their replies.

Undeniably, the driving force behind my search was emotional rather than rational. There had been such an accumulation of suppressed fear and conflict that it affected my judgement – the emotional instability of my childhood, the uncertainty and lack of confidence in my inter-reactions with others, plus the isolating tendencies of those intermittent and distressing bouts of depression. As a consequence, there were times when I probably hindered the steady or logical progress of my quest. I would become unbearably frustrated at the time it all seemed to take, and found myself doing the strangest things just in order to do something, *anything*. At other times a great fear would hold me back from making the very move that could take me forward, for my concern over causing the children (who were so important) any sort of pain, made me fear the contact that I so desperately sought. I was constantly juggling with a spectrum of strong and sometimes conflicting emotions.

But at the same time, enthusiasm was running without check, like a train without a driver. I felt unable to control the extremes of emotion and thoughts bubbling up through the subconscious and taking over such a large part of my daily life. It was as thought I was a passenger on an extraordinary journey which was going to continue, once started, whether it was my wish or not.

There was a feeling of unreality about it all. I was aware of that part of me which was Mary, as always, but now it shared my mind in a way that perhaps it had never done before. There was also awareness of my own needs, but I could not be a complete person without trying to satisfy the needs, relating to that which was Mary. Memory of events in Mary's life began to find their way back into my conscious mind on a daily basis, much as they had in childhood. I was spending a lot of time concentrating on the children's faces and remembering their personalities; they were becoming more familiar again.

Ideas and thought released by the hypnosis began to stay so near the surface that they became more a part of me than they had for many years. The compartmentalising that had taken so long to develop was breaking down. Again I was going through the torments of separation from the children. Logic told me that they had long since grown up and had lived their own lives for many decades, but I needed to know what had happened so that I could allow them to grow up in my memory as they had done in reality.

Although I was excited by taking the first steps in my quest, I was also dubious. There were still so many uncertainties. The hypnosis was undoubtedly helping, but how far could I trust what it was dredging up? There was a consciousness that, although it was revealing a lot I had not remembered, this new knowledge lacked the fine detail which I believed necessary to a successful search. Each time I was hypnotised I *saw* a great deal but did not actually record it in words – usually because I was not asked about it, or because I was asked the wrong question. My own natural taciturnity may also have had a lot to do with it, and I am sure the tapes must have contained gaps and silences in between the questions and occasional answers. If I had not deliberately made as many notes as I could once I got home from the sessions, I'm sure I would have gained almost nothing.

For instance, in one of the sessions I had a very clear picture of an animal trapped. The older boys, and perhaps one of the older girls, had set a snare. This was fairly late, because the oldest boy was about eleven. The snare was checked every day, and one morning they rushed in, all talking together about having caught something. All the children ran out to take a look, and I remember being last out because my hands were wet and were still being dried on a cloth as I joined the group. I looked over the heads gathered round the snare and saw a hare. It was caught by the lower part of its body, so that it looked very long and thin. It must have been a cool day or fairly early, because my hands remained feeling damp and cool, as did the cloth on which they had been dried. The trap had been set by a group of trees and undergrowth close to the cottage. I think the hare was still alive, but could not be certain. I 'saw' all this in my head, and recorded it later, but I know that all I said out loud was: 'It's still alive!'

The fact that I was able to give broad pictures but no fine detail was confined to an extent by something the hypnotist had done at the previous session. He wanted to test my psychic sense – the ability to see things not visible in an ordinary way, or to know things through clairvoyance. I was still under hypnosis when he brought me back to the present but did not wake me. He asked me to 'move up' towards the ceiling and stop near and above a tall cupboard. He had perhaps been influenced by my out-of-the-body experience as Mary, after her death, when I looked down at her husband. The feeling was similar to that of psychometry, in which it is possible for the mind to see through walls, pass through them and describe what lies beyond. (In the past I had had many of my descriptions of this kind confirmed, so I trust their accuracy.)

I saw the cupboard as if from above. He told me that he had put something there and asked me to describe it. I saw the rectangular shape of the top of the cupboard, and on it two flattish square shapes, each covering one side of the top, and each the size of a gramophone record but thicker. Another shape which I saw there was a long cardboard or paper tube stretching the length of the top. Then the hypnotist woke me, and I struggled back to the consciousness.

He had put a small coin in a box that he hoped I would find, but I had not picked up on such fine detail. The record-sized square shapes were in fact two record decks, and the tube he had completely forgotten about. It was a rolled-up poster which could not be seen at all from below in the room.

As a test of clairvoyance under hypnosis this was merely interesting. But as a test of the accuracy of the information that I was giving generally under hypnosis it was quite valuable, confirming my ability to give broad outlines and pictures which lacked fine detail. I felt this could apply to the regression as well: I could 'see' Mary, her children, the cottage, the village – but I could not 'see' names of people or roads, nor dates, with any assured accuracy.

Of the details consistent within both the memory I have always had and the one given under hypnosis, the most reliable was the name itself, Mary. I was quite sure that would turn out to be right. The two principal geographical areas of the memories seemed to be fairly close to each other, and were both north of Dublin: one was the parents' home and village – although I did not know its name – and the other was Malahide. There may have been other places, but not for long periods of time.

In the parents' home there were memories of Mary's father and of two older brothers, who left home some time during Mary's teenage years and went some distance away. I had no concept of their surname. The Letts' house, near to Mary's family home, and where I saw her working, was only seen under hypnosis. It was there that I saw Mary in about 1919 with her husband. The idea that he was not a local man and may well have fought in the First World War was present in both memories and hypnosis; as was the consciousness of his work involving timbers and being up high, and basic personality details. Every time I thought of him, whether as Mary in my own life or as Mary under hypnosis, the memories were the same. They were clear at an early point but were blotted out at a later stage, and I did not know why. I saw the young man, extremely attractive, and in that memory there were all sorts of feelings which were uplifting. But later there were the children and different feelings, the most overriding of which was a sense of quiet caution.

I continually found that I was trying to justify or tolerate his problems even though it was no longer necessary. I wondered about the motivation behind this. He enjoyed attention, yet was unable to open up about worries or concerns. Mary was preoccupied with the children and seemed to have little time to think about him, or had given up trying to understand. His attitude towards the children, which varied between indifference and hostility, could have been partly caused by their receiving his wife's time and attention in a way that he could not.

But I felt there was another side to his personality that was rarely seen – that had been there at the beginning, but was buried along with too much of himself. I wondered about the effect that the war might have had on him. His life seemed to have been a disappointment much of the time. He was preoccupied with working, from which I think he derived some satisfaction, but he was seldom at home. As a young man he was self-confident and noticeable, but he became a man of fewer and fewer words as he seemed to become less happy with life: surly and withdrawn, not really good company at home, though perhaps better amongst his friends.

I was still very unsure about his name as given under hypnosis. Later the hypnotist agreed that it would probably be wrong – too similar to the American film star Ryan O'Neal.

The cottage in Malahide was always the most consistent feature. Of all the details, this struck me as perhaps the most reliable. The descriptions of the children were consistent, too, although their numbers were not. There seemed to be a minimum of five, but I was sure there might have been as many as eight. In an early written record I had mentioned eight children, but when hypnotised I seemed to describe only about five. Under hypnosis, four of the children were given names, but my response to the questions was so casual that I had as many doubts about these names – James, Mary, Harry and Kathy – as I did about Mary's husband's name. The dead baby boy, whom I saw under hypnosis only, perhaps in the early 1930s, was, I felt, the last but one child. The butcher's shop and the church were seen only under hypnosis.

The general dates and timescale were so consistent that I felt they could be relied upon, in which case Mary's death occurred in the 1930s when she was in her mid-thirties. I know nothing of the family after her death, which was how it should be to remain consistent with my assertion that my memories were Mary's.

★

With such total absorption in and preoccupation with the beginnings of the research, my time was spent constantly going over and over the details to see what might be done to find out more. No part of any day was left untouched by the need to find out. There was little else in the content of my conversation, an obsession that others could well have found irritating – and indeed I worried about it. But I was unable to stop thinking and talking about it even for the sake of those around me.

Not many people have the chance to answer a dream, quite literally. There was a sense of being very much alive, a new exuberant reality. Untroubled as yet by a lack of replies from the letters sent to various O'Neils, I began to rush about looking for things to do and enquiries to make. I recognised in myself again that emotionally driven impulsiveness which was so unlikely to achieve careful work and positive results.

The library became a frequent haunt; not only did it contain telephone books for the whole of Ireland, but also reference books which gave useful addresses such as those of records offices. On one occasion I looked up the name Lett. There were several listed in the area, but there was no real need to follow this up; although it was a useful piece of information to know, there was no guarantee that the name had been used correctly. In other words, I now had confirmation that it was a local name, one that Mary might have known or heard, but with my inability to remember names properly it was unwise to assume that it was the right one for the farmhouse's occupants.

Through another of these library visits, I discovered that many files in the Dublin Records Office had been destroyed by fire during the uprising of 1922. These, I realised, might include some that would have been of use to me. However, I thought it would make sense at this point to try to trace a more recent record – perhaps Mary's death certificate. The accuracy of the details was still in question, but initiating a search was better than doing nothing.

I also found out that records were held by priests, so this might be another avenue to explore. I therefore tried to identify the church that I had seen under hypnosis; when I found what I thought must be the correct one – the church on the main road in Malahide – in the telephone directory, I wrote a letter to the priest in charge, outlining the problem much as I had done to the O'Neils. It was only much later, when my letter was returned, that I noticed I had misread the address. By that time I was once again deep in uncertainties, primarily about the surname, and I felt that I was perhaps clutching at straws. Deep down I knew that there was a strong chance I was off-centre with the information I was using.

Finally I investigated the cost of travel to Dublin, which would enable me to ask about the family in the village where they had lived. To fly would be quickest and would cause minimum disruption to domestic life. I knew it would cost too much for the whole family to go, but at the same time I hated the idea of being parted from them – not a surprising admission, since the whole basis of my search was to do with separation from children. However, I still could not afford to go, even alone, so I abandoned the idea.

Waiting for replies to letters which might in any case not be answered became an intolerable effort. Hyperactivity created a false impression of the passage of time. I performed a juggling act between trying to suppress most of my ebullience and channelling those energies into productive avenues – but it was mostly unsuccessful. My mind wanted to rest and be free at the same time as it wanted to work and be productive, but could do or be neither. I knew that I must find the family or try to forget them. Remembering, but not being able to find them, would become unbearable.

It seemed important constantly to remind myself that there were others like me somewhere, but the well-documented studies of children whose pre-life memories had been scientifically checked made me feel inadequate. When I had first read about them I wondered if I should contact the researcher, Dr Stevenson, but I felt that my inability to remember names properly would mean that nobody would be sufficiently interested to help.

In some cases families were found, and that should have made it easier for me. But such cases tended to be used with a view to proving reincarnation (which I believe cannot be proved in retrospect); and the fact that the discussions did not include the feelings of the principals concerned, or the way they coped with their memories, offered me little comfort.

Once again I began to think of why and how I had the memories, to try to rationalise the means by which they had become mine. There are several views on the subject. One is that it may be an 'echo' of a memory collected at around the time of birth. As I have always had several such memories, in order for this theory to work they would have had to be collected as memories in sequence, and they certainly do seem to come with a gap of up to eight years between each. It is not a theory I would agree with, and seems clumsy. The other main option is that the memories are of previous lives and run in sequence because they are a continuation of the same essential 'soul' or 'person'. However hard this idea may be to accept, if it is viewed entirely logically, without emotive rejection, it is viable.

The third view I have heard put forward is that it is a collection of ideas collated through listening to other people and assembled into a sort of 'pseudo-memory'. Unfortunately for this hypothesis, I did not have a series of historians discussing various periods of time whilst I sat in my pram. And, as it happens, my own knowledge of, and interest in, history is embarrassingly poor. So far as my main memories are concerned, my family knew nobody from Malahide, and their first thoughts on the family I remembered were initiated by me. I clung to the statistically unlikely accuracy of the hand-drawn map, which was probably the most interesting confirmed detail to date, and which could not have been produced from imagination. It is highly unlikely that I would have studied such a map as a baby. This particular hypothesis leans towards being an explanation contrived after the event, and does not make full analytical use of the information on past life memories.

It was with myself that I argued – it was my own need to be certain, my own confusion that needed to be satisfied, the gnawing concern over Mary's family driving me on to find answers. Because the memory was now so much at the front of my mind, there was a feeling that I had neglected what should have been done a long time before: the search should have been carried out much sooner. Yet I also wondered at the mystery of fate that had led to my searching at a time when I had a family of my own and when the feelings associated with children were in my daily experience.

I felt a tremendous guilt that I had not done the memories of Mary justice. If the wish was to be sure that the children were all right, then it had taken too long. They would now be in their sixties or so, and would have come to terms with their past. I did not see that I could be of any value to them. Only the thought that perhaps the search had *had* to wait until this time could stem my feelings of failure and worthlessness. I was now about the same age as Mary at the time of her death. I had children, and had experienced some quite severe problems in my life that might help me to understand a little better the family that was left behind. The memories I had were of a worthy woman, and perhaps now I could deem myself worthy enough to carry her memory with me.

*

At the next hypnosis session I was plunged once more into my mind's depths; memories were plundered and fragments were captured and exposed like paper in the wind. This time I was more self-critical, less detached; I was finding the whole thing too traumatic, too disturbing.

The touch on my shoulder directed me back to 1850; then I was asked to describe what I could see. There was a ship with three sails. My voice mumbled as the scene slowly opened out. I tried to see all that was possible so that I could paint the picture in detail. The hypnotist asked questions, but my response was poor at first, as always tended to happen if the hypnosis was very deep. However, I managed to describe the life of a girl of about fifteen named Jane Matthews, living in Southampton. I mentioned a street name and gave details of the dockside to the west of the city. I described a flower-seller, dock-workers, sailors, a father who was violent, a small terraced house with two rooms and no windows at the back, and a life ended as a runaway, hiding in a barn with the horses.

We went forward again, this time to 1922. It was early in the year, and the hypnotist asked me about the Troubles in Ireland, but I did not understand. There was always trouble somewhere, angry people. He asked me to try to look as though from the outside, like watching a film, but I was unable to do so – I could only see the memory through Mary's eyes. I actually *lived* the memory; I did not just view it as though I were a spectator.

He asked me about the Letts, but I knew little. I volunteered that I thought they had moved away. He asked me about this, hoping to gain some information relating to the Troubles, but as Mary, in the divided state of mind that I found under hypnosis, it was not there to give. Mary was fairly insular, and more bothered by her own family and problems.

I was asked about the church where the children were baptised, but I couldn't find a name. There was a query about a priest, and I was not sure; but there was a name in my mind – Michael. (This was one of the points on which I was later to question the validity of the details given under hypnosis. My older brother Michael, a padre in the RAF, was killed in a gliding accident when he was thirty-four, and thoughts of him and his priesthood were bound to be lodged in my subconscious, particularly as loss was still not an experience I felt able to face properly.) I could not know where the truth might lie.

There were questions about the cottage. The name of the road it was in began with the letter S – something like 'Salmons'. It was rented from a man nicknamed Mac. I had other images, about his working along the coast. When asked, I was not sure if Mac had other properties. There were many questions about a variety of things, some of which I as my present self would have been able to answer, yet as Mary could not. That was confusing in itself and puzzled me.

I was instructed to go to the happiest memory of Mary's life. Immediately I saw the birth of her first son. What had he expected? I wondered. He asked more questions, silly questions, and there was some impatience and a little sarcasm in the replies.

He took me back further again, this time to 1650. There was a large barn and I was aware of watching men working, and sawdust on the floor, but was completely unable to understand what they were doing. *Too* completely, for there was a level of incomprehension that was abnormal. There was a sense of isolation, of something wrong, of difficulty in communication. It was a boy of maybe ten, but with an odd feeling of being alone. Perhaps deaf, I thought later, or autistic. I was taken away from this time before it was possible to understand more. It was difficult to communicate with the hypnotist, and he had no way of knowing that I was seeing something even though I could not talk about it or describe it.

Struggling to wake again was always hard. There was much to discuss, but at this point I was to have a break from hypnosis for a couple of months. This was immensely frustrating so far as the search was concerned, but at the same time something of a relief. The hypnotist thought I should avoid becoming too wrapped up in the experience. I wanted to deny that it was too much to handle, but it was not until later that I realised just how involved and affected I had been.

Because I felt I needed to do something, I continued in my efforts to research the family. I telephoned the first Mr O'Neil to whom I had written, as I could not cope with the lack of replies. It is not in my nature to push people, so I felt uncomfortable about it, but as things turned out he was quite interested and helpful.

'Oh yes, we've been asking around and there was a family on the Dublin road whom it could have been,' he said.

'The Dublin road?' I replied. 'No, I'm pretty sure that the family I'm looking for lived on the road to Swords, as on the map I sent.'

He said that he could not quite place the roads on the map, but offered to do some searching. I felt that if he were going to do anything for me I had to be honest about my reasons. So in answer to his question about my connection to the family, I told him that it was a little odd and not easy to explain – that the map and other details had come in part from dreams I'd had since childhood.

He went very quiet, and then said, 'You're joking!'

I felt extremely embarrassed and rather foolish, but managed to explain that so far a few things had turned out to be correct, like the map. I told him also about the baby boy, the last child but one, who had died at birth. He had the patience to listen, but with obvious reservations. Telephones have never been my favourite means of communicating. It is much easier to judge situations and responses face to face, and to modify explanations. I had written letters because I knew that on paper it was easier to be careful about what I said. Now, on the telephone to Mr O'Neil, I had been caught unawares and had just started to talk about Mary, forgetting that this was something out of the ordinary.

I started to feel a little paranoid. I should have anticipated Mr O'Neil's reaction, and as I had still received no reply to any of the other letters I envisaged all the people I had written to in the Malahide area getting together and deciding that the whole thing was too bizarre to warrant any response. This might jeopardise further research.

However, a day or so later Mr O'Neil rang back. He had looked again at my hand-drawn map and checked the details against a street map of Malahide. He had found my map to be more accurate than he had expected, given that it had been drawn from dreams. He again offered to help, and I felt considerably better about having been honest with him. Just being aware that, after his initial doubt, he had realised there was some possible truth in what I was doing gave me confidence.

On hearing of the existence of the Malahide street map, I wrote straight off to the Irish Tourist Board. Soon I was looking at a very detailed map of the place, and everything I knew about it sprang into greater prominence. As before, the railway and the churches were marked. The road with the church I had seen under hypnosis – as well as the butcher's shop – was actually called Church Road! The main road running east to West was The Mall, later becoming the Dublin Road which ran south to the city. The jetty on to the estuary was clearly visible and Gaybrook – a name that meant something to me, thought I was not sure what – was just where the cottage had been.

Best of all, though, I now had the name of Mary's road. It was not Salmons, but Swords Road (fairly obvious, actually, as it led to the village of Swords). However, it was an enormous step forward and offered great hope because, although it was only an approximation (in the sense of the S at the beginning of the name), it was about as close as I usually get when trying to remember names.

Now I could see how my whole approach to finding the family could change direction. Instead of relying on the surname of the family – about which I was very unsure anyway – it would be far better to go back to basics and try to trace the family who had lived in the first cottage on the left on Swords Road. If, when I found them, the details of their family history seemed to fit, I could go on to see whether any of their personal memories matched mine. It was important to be right, so the correspondences would have to be extremely good before either I or that family would be satisfied: without the assurance of the correct surname, everything else would have to correlate to a point where there could be no doubt.

Using only the memories from my childhood, I wanted first to find out who had lived in the cottage fifty years before, and then go carefully step by step. Because I was still unable to follow up this line of research in person, I had to think of ways to ask questions at a distance, and whom to ask.

First of all I collated all the queries I had that could easily be answered, and compiled a kind of questionnaire. This included information gleaned from the new street map, for there were of course many more roads marked on it than on my childhood map. I presumed that those near Swords Road were of housing estates – had they drained the marshes?

I hoped to be able to find someone who was willing and able to track down the answers. But I have never liked asking people to do things for me, so I kept the list short and simple. If I could get some sort of lead I could take over and do the

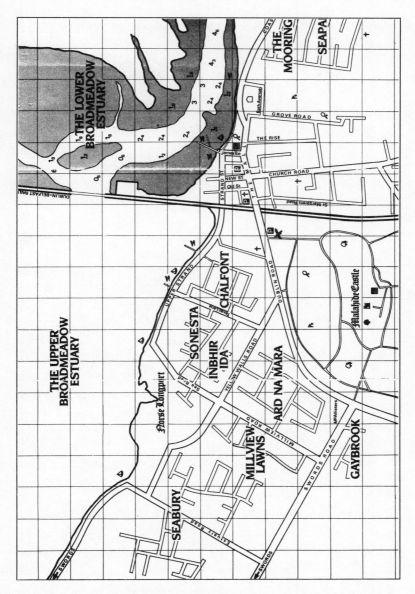

Malahide street map (Malahide Sports & Leisure, distributed by Malahide Chamber of Commerce).

bulk of the work myself. I thought about who could answer some of the questions – local historical societies, the Rotary Club, women's groups and the local council – or perhaps I could find a volunteer. The questionnaire read as follows:

It may not be possible to answer all of the questions, but any answers found will be helpful.

1. *Is there a cottage still standing at the position marked on the map enclosed?*
2. *If there is, what would be the approximate age of the building?*
3. *Was there a cottage in that position in the 1920s?*
4. *If there was, is it possible to find out the name of the family who lived there in the 1920s?*
5. *Judging by the style of housing, is it likely that the housing areas were built before or after 1940?*
                    Seabury
                    Millview Lawns
                    Ard Na Mara
6. *If it is possible, could you find out anything about the history of any family that may have lived in the cottage in the position marked on the photocopied map of Malahide, and enclose it when returning this questionnaire? I believe there were five to eight children, and that the mother, Mary, died some time in the 1930s.*
7. *Is it possible to give a description of the three churches in Malahide?*

I thank you for any help that you are able to give towards my search. I realise that some of the questions may require more work than is reasonable, so I don't expect everything to be answered.

While deciding who to send copies of the questionnaire to, I composed an advertisement for the Irish supplement to the *Mensa Magazine*, published by British Mensa Limited, an organisation to which I had belonged since 1988. It read: 'Help needed in a limited amount of research of an unusual nature in the Malahide area.'

As my excitement grew – I seemed at last to be getting somewhere – I grew more reluctant to be hypnotised again. As the time drew nearer I felt I really did not want to go through it again. As this was to be the last session, I realised that it was necessary to check on the answers and see if they were the same, but I was reticent. The research itself was nowhere near finished – in fact, it had barely started – but it could be followed up without going through any more hypnosis. I began to view it as an ordeal, and wondered if it was such a good idea to continue. However, the arrangements had been made, and I knew that this part of the research should be completed if it was to be of any value. The break had given me the chance to stand back a little and be realistic about the effect the hypnosis had on me.

Surprisingly, I found that I was more relaxed than usual, though the session was confusing. It was a matter of going back over dates and names, so there was a lot of changing about from place to place and time to time. Most of the names were the same, but there were some changes – enough to make me suspicious about the names in general. My main concern after the session was that I might be remembering what I had said before rather than remembering within the memories themselves.

When it was all over, I felt as though I had been left almost where I was before the hypnosis started. I had a family to find, who lived at a specific location, about whom I had details relating to personal history, but no names that I could rely on, or at least no definite surname.

Perhaps the biggest difficulty with the hypnosis was that I had wanted to find out more about Mary, whereas the hypnotist had wanted to research hypnotic regression. The result of any enterprise where there is a conflict of interest, even when each party is trying to help the other, is that neither is served particularly well. I cannot deny that I had fallen on the offer of hypnosis like a drowning woman: it seemed like an extraordinarily valuable opportunity to be grasped. It was an experience that I will not forget and do not want to, despite the lack of concrete details such as that forever elusive surname. The fact that other memories were also examined was of interest and benefit.

The search for Mary's family would still have to rely on the details that have been present with me from childhood. It would have been possible to have conducted the research without the hypnosis, yet some of the details that arose helped complete the picture, and several were very useful in confirming that I did know things about the family that nobody outside the family could know. The hypnosis also played a large part in increasing my motivation and confidence, without which the search might not have been possible.

I still had had no response to any of the other O'Neil letters, nor from the Records Office in Dublin. I did, however, meet someone whom Mr Coulter had talked about − Colin Skinner, a friend of his who was studying theology in Dublin. He had previously been a history teacher with a strong interest in Irish history, and was most interested in helping. He took back with him to Dublin a copy of the hand-drawn map, all the details I knew about the family and where they lived, and the questionnaire. I also gave him the description and drawing of the church I had described under hypnosis − the one with the large gable and with coping stones; I

Left: The Rotunda Hospital, Dublin, where Mary died in 1932. This picture shows the tall windows which I vividly remembered.

Right: New Street, Malahide, circa 1920.
(The Malahide Historical Society)

Left: The jetty, Malahide, where I remember standing at dusk, waiting for a boat to return.

Right: There is still a butcher's shop in Malahide where I described. Mary passed this shop often but could not afford to buy meat.

*Above: With Mary's eldest child,
Sonny, at our first meeting
in September 1990.*

*Right: The four brothers when
first reunited in 1985.
From left: Jeffrey,
Christy, Frank and Sonny.*

*Left: Mary's eldest daughter, Mary,
who died in 1946 aged 24.*

*Below: With Phyllis at
Dublin airport
in February 1993.*

Right: Mary with Phyllis aged 2 in 1927.

Left: This Malahide cottage is reminiscent of Mary's home with its central fireplace and two rooms. (The Malahide Historical Society)

Right: The ruins of Gaybrook Lodge photographed in February 1993. All that remained were crumbling stone walls enclosing a dark, damp interior, still recognisable, however, despite the decay.

Above: St Andrew's Church, Church Street, Malahide, which Mary passed on the way to visit her sister.

Below: A drawing of St Andrew's Church which I did from my description under hypnosis in 1988. My positioning of the church on the west side of Church Street was also correct.

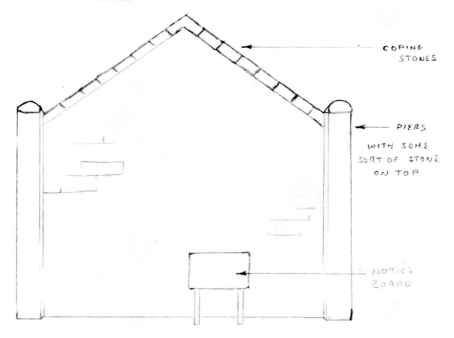

still thought that this was where the family records might be held.

Mr Skinner asked if he might use the memories as part of a thesis towards his qualification, as they brought up a number of ideas of theological interest. This did not worry me, as I have always been happy to accept that there are a variety of views on and answers to any situation. For him to look at the information and discuss it from his standpoint could only be to the good, even if it turned out that he was totally opposed to my beliefs.

I also thought it was a good idea to share the research, since independent checking would leave less room for mistakes or misinterpretations, as I was still uncertain about so much and wondered if I really had enough detail to go ahead properly. Although other people's confidence in me helped, it also increased my sense of responsibility to carry out the task properly. Sometimes it felt that the reality of now was as fragile as those memories of yesterday.

Then I got an answer to the advertisement in the club magazine. A freelance journalist who lived in Swords, the next town to Malahide, answered saying that she was constantly doing research and a little more would be no problem. I wrote her a letter in reply.

Dear ——,

Thank you for your offers of help. First, please may I apologise that I am only able to offer limited expenses and not a payment as such.

I am looking for some answers to the enclosed questionnaire in the search for a family who lived in Malahide. It is difficult that I do not as yet have the surname with any certainty.

Also, before I can ask you to do anything, to be fair, I must explain why the research is unusual because you may feel that you would rather not be involved. This is 'past life memory research', however that may be interpreted.

If you do want to help I would willingly explain myself further should you wish.
> *Thank you.*
> *Yours sincerely,*
> *Jenny Cockell*

I never heard from her again.

Time passed, very little progress was being made, and there was little feedback from the new contacts – and nothing at all from any of those to whom I had written. It was still possible that I was researching in the wrong way, or that I was relying too much on details given under hypnosis – the dubious surname, for instance. What I really needed was to make contact with someone who had lived in Malahide for a number of years and could remember the families who had lived there in the 1920s and 1930s. Ideally I needed to go there myself, but at this time we could not even afford family holidays, so such a visit was ruled out.

The waiting was thoroughly frustrating and depressing, but there was also a positive side. Having started the search after so many years of wishing but not feeling able to do anything about it, everything had been brought to the surface and memories had crowded in, pushing all else out of perspective. And, just as problems seem easier after a good night's sleep, time as a healer had given me a better perspective on the memories. They had settled into my life at a more conscious level, but were no longer as disturbing as they had been during the hypnotic regression. I could cope a little better with waiting. I would not give up, and would think of as many ways as possible to complete the search, but in the meantime I was more able to continue with normal life.

Nevertheless, despite my optimism, as the end of 1988 approached I began to slow down. The hyperactivity – as well as the stress of the hypnosis – had worn me out. My metabolism swung into a weary lower gear, and as winter began I entered an almost hibernatory state. I knew that little could be done for several months because I would have neither energy nor enthusiasm until I was relieved of this bout of depression. This was the worst I had felt for many years. In the end I had to resort, for the first time in my life, to chemical correction through medication. I had reached my lowest ebb.

5

Malahide
at Last

Just as I was beginning to think that life was a bottomless
pit of black misery, and that all my hopes were impossible
to achieve, something changed. In January 1989, completely
out of the blue, I was offered quite a lot more work – from a
state-registered chiropodist who was moving away. For years I
had been trying to build up my workload and thus my income,
but had found it slow going. I was still working part-time
for the Health Authority, but needed to increase the private
side. Now, suddenly, I had a chance to get ahead.

Within a couple of months, during which my depression
lifted slowly and my earnings grew, one thing became clear:
I was going to be able to visit Malahide. Having discussed
it with my husband, the money was put aside and the trip
arranged for the first weekend in June. Well in advance I
booked cheap weekend flights – out to Dublin from Luton
Airport on Friday the 2nd at 6.30 p.m., and back at 4.30 p.m.
on Sunday the 4th. I booked myself into a modest hotel, the
Grove, at the eastern end of Malahide, which had been on
a list sent by the Irish Tourist Board along with the street

map. Effectively I was going to have less than two days in Malahide, but I could not afford to stay any longer and in any case did not want to be away from my family for too long.

At last I was going to visit the place where Mary had lived – where *I* had lived in my memories of her – and have the chance to get some truths confirmed. I had pictures in my head that had been with me since childhood, and had gained additional memories and insight from the hypnosis sessions. Now I would be able to see for myself.

It was not just the money that had prevented me going sooner, although that was a major factor – it was also a matter of justifying the expense. I had to believe in myself enough. The feelings that had dominated me for the past few years since the birth of my children, and the hypnosis during the previous year, had been necessary before I could accept that this was more than a wild goose chase. Despite the health setbacks, as I had grown more confident so I had grown into my quest. All at once there seemed to be a kind of sense behind all those months of trying, of waiting in vain, and all the subsequent frustration and depression. I felt that this had all needed to happen in order to create sufficient motivation in me to take this psychologically huge – and expensive – step.

Despite the shortness of the visit, the potential benefits were obvious. The main one as far as I was concerned was that I would be able to walk around looking for specific details and landmarks from my original memories or which had been described under hypnosis. Second, actually being there might provoke new memories to make the jigsaw more complete, and thus help in the search for Mary's family. I would also be able to take photographs, which could prove useful. And I might even meet someone from my other past. . . .

Much more needed to be checked than could possibly be done in a weekend, so I had to decide on priorities and hope to cover the most important areas. There would be no time to check records or names – and of course I was still not confident about the surname O'Neil. In any case, places which might hold records – council offices, local libraries and so on – would most likely be closed over the weekend.

I found myself constantly going over in my mind the places that needed to be seen and recorded, and wrote innumerable lists. The cottage in Swords Road was the first priority as it held a dominant place in my memory. I even started to have dreams about it – that it had been pulled down and that only the foundations remained, hidden beneath clumps of grass and buttercups. Funnily enough, there were always people with me during these dreams – for once I was not alone.

The church in Church Road was the second clearest picture in my mind; I hoped to compare it with my mental picture and with the drawing I had made and copied for the theology student. The butcher's shop, the jetty and the railway station were other elements of my mind knowledge of Malahide. Would the rest of the village seem as familiar to me?

I had waited all my life to be able to go on this trip – by many people's standards a very short one. I feared failure or disappointment, but also success. I realised that success could bring its own problems, and stresses for myself and the family if they were found. What I expected to achieve was partial and limited answers, but also many more questions. I had to dissuade myself from being swamped by too much hope or expectation.

Stress can cause physical illness. During the week leading up to the trip I suffered a severe recurrence of a back condition; for several days I was only able to crawl a short distance in considerable pain, and was quite unable to stand up. As the weekend in Malahide was to involve a great deal of walking I expected to have to cancel my plans. However, after a particularly painful and sleepless night, most of which was spent on the floor forcing my spine against the hard surface, I was once again able to stand.

This was the Thursday, the day before the flight. Something strange had happened while I lay on the floor: tiredness and pain had lifted me into an odd frame of mind, slightly detached. I felt, fatalistically, that if I was meant to go to Ireland I would be able to stand up in the morning. If I could not stand, I would have to accept that the trip was not meant to take place and that the search for Mary's children was not intended to go any further. So when I found I could stand I took it as confirmation that I was doing the right thing.

That day I got some medication from the doctor, followed by, the next day, the services of a physiotherapist who manipulated me so that I could walk a little. I did not admit to either that I was planning to fly to Ireland for the weekend, but after exercise I was just about able to carry a small bag and remain seated for a time. I was not comfortable, but I was not going to miss this opportunity.

The plane was delayed. I had not flown for sixteen years, and had forgotten about waiting in a busy airport lounge for flight announcements. In my nervousness and excitement, I engaged the young man next to me in conversation. It was perhaps as well that he was happy to talk, as it could easily have spoiled his journey if he had hoped for a quiet flight. I could not believe that at last I was making the trip, and so I wanted to share with anyone who would listen the feelings and emotions churning around in my mind: externalising ideas makes it easier to put them into perspective.

The taxi driver at the airport in Dublin had no idea where the hotel or the road was, so I directed him from the street map. It was not far from the airport to Malahide and the journey only took about ten minutes. He drove to Swords first and then turned right towards Malahide, along the very lane in which I felt the family had lived. It was a dull, wet evening, but that hardly mattered since I was so excited by the whole adventure. As we went over a small bridge – over my stream? – I strained to see if there were any old buildings left that might possibly be the cottage I wanted to find. I caught a brief glimpse of one likely candidate, on the right side of the road and in the hoped for style and position. But there was little time to look back through the rain-drenched rear window as it passed out of sight.

When the taxi reached the hotel it was twilight, and by the time I had some coffee and sandwiches it was completely dark. So, despite my overwhelming enthusiasm, there was no point in trying to do anything that night. I went stiffly to bed, but slept very little. I was in Malahide at last!

On the Saturday morning I started out quite early. No staff were about in the hotel, and as I did not want to disturb anyone or wait until they got up and unlocked the front door, I let myself out at the side door. It locked automatically behind me, so I knew it would be a while before I could return. With a rucksack on my back containing sandwiches, camera, notebook and map, I set off eagerly. The nearest mental landmark was the jetty, so I turned out of Grove Road into James Terrace.

The jetty itself turned out to be quite modern, but might have replaced an older one. It was made of concrete, while the jetty of memory was wooden-boarded. A small fishing boat was moored there, and a fisherman was sorting through some pots. The coastline curved away to the east out of the estuary and towards the open sea. I was disturbingly aware of a strong and ridiculously comforting sense of familiarity and, although struggling to remain objective, I was aware of the need for details that could be confirmed. As I stood there I remembered yet again waiting at dusk, wrapped inadequately in a black shawl as the cold sea breeze blew inland. I still could not remember the person for whom I was waiting. Often I had rationalised to myself that perhaps Mary's father or her husband was at sea, though that awareness was not really present or very strong. I had thought that, if the husband were a sailor or fisherman, that would explain why he was out of the house for such long periods of time. But as I stood there that idea just did not feel right, and I began to think that it was not him whom I remembered waiting for. It was important not to interpret the memories, but just to accept the fragments as they stood and try to fit the pieces together when the missing parts emerged.

However, feelings were not going to be enough; I had to try to find something more substantial, if possible, so I moved on. I looked for the wooden gates I remembered, but there seemed to be no trace of them. I wondered if I had their location wrong in my head. I then turned left into Church Road, which I had mentioned under hypnosis and marked on my childhood maps. It was the north-to-south road in the middle of Malahide, and I knew there were a number of shops at the north end of it. Most of the buildings were old and many had obviously been shops for quite some time. But it was only under hypnosis that I had described the butcher's shop, which was on the west side, about second or third from the corner at the north end.

As I looked across the street it was quite clear that there was still a butcher's shop in the same position. It was stone-built and of some age − certainly old enough to have been standing at the time I remembered. The front had been rendered, but the render was beginning to chip away at the corners to reveal the ageing stone beneath. Older windows had been replaced by large modern ones, but otherwise it looked virtually the same. When I asked in the shop how long it had been a butcher's, they said they thought it must have been at least sixty years.

Suddenly my excitement and optimism were raised to fever pitch by this confirmation that it had been there in Mary's time, plus the simple fact that I had described it and its location accurately *and* recognised it. I had not expected to find anything quite so accurate as this. Maybe I had become so used to not being able to do anything about tracing the family that my level of expectation had dropped too far. But now I was standing looking at a real building that until this point in time I had only seen with my mind. Relief surged up in me.

As I stood there, my heart thudding as adrenalin pumped through my veins, thoughts came to me of Mary shopping. Quite why I remembered the butcher's shop I do not know, as there was never enough money to buy meat from it. Any meat we had was usually rabbit or wild birds caught in the snares the children would set in the fields. As my mind scampered across the memory of cooking a stew containing more potatoes than meat, I felt a frisson of fear that it would not be ready in time. In time for what?

Suppressing the memory − why was it of *fear*? − I decided to go further along Church Road and see if I could recognise the church. The first of three to check, it was on the west side, the same side as the butcher's shop. As I walked I felt an overwhelming sense that this was a road travelled regularly in Mary's life; the older buildings looked very familiar. And when I reached the church itself I stopped, spellbound.

Under hypnosis I had given a fairly detailed description of the outside of the building − and I had later drawn it − but with my usual lack of confidence I had anticipated only a rough similarity. But here before me was the large gable end I had described, flat and undecorated, with coping stones along the top and an integral pillar at each end topped with a stone. In front was a notice-board. This was not the old wooden one I had remembered, but could easily have been a replacement in a similar position. The parts of the church that I had not described were those further from the road, which only came properly into view when you entered. This increased my feeling that it was a building regularly passed rather than entered. But where had Mary been going? So far as I could remember, there was little of interest in her life in that direction.

The church – St Andrew's – was Church of Ireland, much as I had expected, and so would not have been the one Mary attended, nor indeed where any of the family records would be. The gable end seen from the road was almost a false front, and was certainly an unusual structural addition, which, having been described in detail, as well as drawn, and its position marked on maps, represented wonderful confirmation of the accuracy of my memories. I found myself trembling with excitement. Now I could accept far more of the details than I had hitherto. I could relax more, because the dreams, the memories and the pictures released by the hypnosis had been shown to be about reality, and so there was a very potent chance of my being able to trace the children.

I could not wait to head for the lane where the cottage was. Without thinking I turned to the left, subconsciously expecting to be able to use a shortcut that I knew to be there. But as I looked along the side of the church, I realised that things had changed. There was a shut gate, with a house further back in the field, making the place look very private. I doubted that this route was any longer a public thoroughfare. I retraced my steps up Church Street instead, intending to check the other churches and the station on the way to Swords Road.

The first church I came to was the large Catholic one, St Sylvester's, which was impressive and ornate, with a garden and large, sweeping drive. As I had always thought of Mary as Catholic, I expected to recognise it, but I did not. I remember *walking* to church as Mary, and the people, so perhaps the building had been less important than the event. I did seem to have a memory of standing talking in front of a church before going for the service, so that could have been there. There was no room in front of St Andrew's for the numbers of people I remembered gathering there.

I stood, hesitant, in front of the church where I knew Mary had worshipped. I wanted to go in, and of course I should have done, but a number of things stopped me. It was so large, people were entering and leaving in a constant stream, and frankly I felt intimidated and out of place. Not only do I have a fear of large numbers of people, but I didn't want to interrupt whatever service was obviously taking place. And the priest would have been fully occupied in any case. This church belonged to my past time, I was no longer part of that faith, and I felt that the truth of my memories could not be accepted there. For, in the sixth century, it became part of Catholic doctrine that a belief in reincarnation was heresy. In my desperate need to respect other people's beliefs, I did not feel I could be welcome there.

Knowing I was perhaps missing out on a huge opportunity, I turned away and walked on along The Mall towards the point where it became the Dublin road. I passed the railway station, the sight of which caused me no surprise: it was as I had described it, set back from the road. There was no really strong sense of familiarity here, just a sense of it being right. The third church, a few yards further on, was a small, very pretty Presbyterian one set back from the road. It was fairly new and would certainly not have been here in the 1920s.

Now at last I could set my sights on the cottage, and I walked almost a mile to the beginning of Swords Road, where I knew it had been. The lane started much as I had remembered it, on the left side anyway. The north, right-hand side was covered with new housing developments, the oldest probably dating back to about the 1950s. And the petrol station on the corner I did not expect at all. The left side of the lane was bordered with ancient hedging and trees for about a hundred yards; then the road widened and there was a new housing development put up in the 1960s or thereabouts.

After these houses, the hedgerows returned and I felt much more comfortable. Behind the hedge were plenty of trees and, in amongst it, remnants of an old stone wall. This was no longer the height of the one I remembered, and the sections were short and falling down. There was a small, gate-sized opening with the remains of stone piers, but I was confused by the changes and felt uncertain. Later I became more sure that this was all that was left for me to find, but that day I was still looking for and hoping to find the cottage standing. For a little while I stood by these remains trying to remember how it had been and if this was the spot, but my mind could not cope with the difference between what I could remember and what was there now. The kaleidoscope of my memories usually contained a detailed and apparently complete picture of the cottage and its surroundings, but in reality there was nothing. I felt a piercing sense of disappointment. Perhaps my dreams of foundations only had been telling me the truth.

On the opposite side of the road there was an old hedge and one remaining boggy meadow; perhaps it had been too wet to drain and build on. The stream ran through the meadow still, so I knew I was on the right spot – the stream was always to the west of the cottage. For that I was thankful, as I had so much wanted to see things I could recognise. I stood looking at the trickle to which the stream had degenerated, and my thoughts turned to the children, particularly to the oldest girl, who would always so patiently and willingly help Mary – fetching water from here, for instance, perhaps from a pump. I felt the familiar flicker of anxiety for her – had she had to take on the role of mother after Mary's death, giving up all her hopes of education and a better life?

Hoping against hope, I crossed the bridge over the stream and approached the old building that I had seen fleetingly from the taxi the night before. Part of me so much wanted it to be the cottage. It *was* the first old building on the left, the distance along the lane was about right and it also stood sideways to the road; but something in the back of my mind kept telling me that it wasn't quite right. The lie of the land at this point was wrong, and there were differences in the building, which was being used as a barn. It also seemed to be too near to the junction with the side road.

However, as it was my only real lead I went nearer to look for someone to talk to. There was a farm just beyond it, which did not appear too modern, but when I crossed the road and walked into the yard I was seen off by two good-sized farm dogs who had no intention of letting anyone come close. I must admit to a certain nervousness of dogs, so I took a few photographs and decided to try a later enquiry by letter: someone might live here who could help. The lane had changed very much more than I had expected, and as this was the only old building it might be the home of someone who had lived here in the 1920s.

Walking back through Malahide to the hotel was both overwhelming and disappointing. The area was full of recent housing developments, typical of any place within easy commuting distance of a major town or city. This made it harder to see how the place might have been; so little of what I remembered had stayed intact.

I walked back past the Catholic church to see if it might be more familiar when approached from the usual direction – from the cottage. But it struck no chords of memory, and still intimidated me, and I wondered, however, whether the frontage had changed in the intervening fifty years or so: the lawns might once have been a graveyard, and the driveway certainly looked new.

As I returned along the Dublin road, a light rain started to fall, refreshing and gentle. A confusion of thoughts rushed around in my head, and as I tried to make some sense of them a new feeling of calm and happiness grew. Across the road from the butcher's shop was a café where a welcome cup of coffee kept me company as I started to write up a few notes on the morning's findings. The fact that I had been able to walk round the village as though I knew it, with the memory of how it was and the present being strangely combined, had not seemed extraordinary. I *did* know the village, although I had only expected to recognise it in part.

When I returned to the hotel at lunchtime, I went to the bar and ordered some sandwiches, which in due course were brought to me by a solidly built man in his early thirties. In a friendly manner, he asked if I were on holiday, and I found myself opening up to him. Once I started to talk, I experienced a great need to unburden myself. Feeling elated by what I had found, I began to explain that I was there to do some personal research, and that I was following up a dream. I said I had memories of a life in Malahide and had drawn maps of the area from early childhood. He enquired if I had been to Malahide before, and I replied that it was my first trip. Then I outlined the story of the memories and told him about the things I had been able to confirm. He was quite fascinated, and interrupted a couple of times to ask me questions such as, 'Would there be a family connection?' or 'How do you think you can know these things?' By the manner of his conversation it seemed that he was quite able to accept that there was something very real and unusual about the research.

Afterwards I worried that I had been too open, but then I realised that our conversation had its advantages – it constituted a kind of proof of my search. All the letters of enquiry, too, that had seemed such a waste of time the previous year, would be evidence of what I was attempting. Going back further in my mind, I became aware of a calendar of events and interactions that could also prove useful from the point of view of proof. I asked my confidant at the hotel if he would have any objection to confirming the content of our conversation should anyone need to check up on my visit, and he did not. This would probably not be necessary, but I felt that all possibilities should be covered.

For the rest of the afternoon I wandered through Malahide, looking again at the places I recognised, letting my mind filter the information, hoping that new pictures or half-forgotten memories would emerge. It crossed my mind that I could have searched for a grave, or graves, but I was not sure where Mary might have been buried – was it in Malahide? – and yet again, I was not sure that the surname I had, O'Neil, was correct.

When I telephoned home my husband said, 'I suppose you've found everything and want to come home now.' I did not realise how much confidence he had in the project. He had expected me to be able to find everything as described, because so many of the earlier things had proved to be right.

Most of the rest of the weekend seemed to be spent walking, looking, feeling and remembering. I had probably done rather too much walking because the backache, which had been under control, returned. Now I just missed my family and wanted to be back with them. I was glad when it was time to ring for a taxi to take me to the airport. I knew that when I returned there would be a great deal of work to do, and I was eager to begin.

What happened during my visit to Malahide was important. At last I had seen and touched some of the things that until then had been just images in my mind; everything suddenly became very real and somehow more valid. At last I felt that there was enough confirmation for me to be able to trust myself and push on in earnest. I had not been aware that I had so little belief in myself. Those close to me had seen this, and it had been their support, their belief in me, that had kept me going.

I was standing in a portal between memory and reality, where it was clear at last that the only gap between the two was of time – both real, but different times. A tension within me had rapidly eased and been replaced by confidence, a much-needed feeling. The whole trip was about feelings – being allowed to heal. It was almost as though I had been hit on the head with all that was around me and told: 'Of course it's all here! Now get on with the job and stop worrying!'

During the weeks that followed, my need to externalise and talk to anyone and everyone about the experience brought a surprisingly positive response. People wanted to hear about it and were interested – which was probably just as well as they were going to hear about it anyway! But I also needed to see if it was possible to discuss the project without causing others to feel uncomfortable because of their own beliefs. It takes most of us a long time to formulate our views of the world, and it was not my place to try to undermine those held by other people.

The encouragement and support were so reassuring that I felt able to discuss aspects previously unvoiced because they had seemed so extreme. Suddenly none of the things that I had half hidden through fear needed to be concealed any more. The ideas and theories involved in reincarnation were a case in point. It struck me that there must be a way of putting forward the phenomenon so that it could be understood within personal frameworks. One day I might have to talk about this with the family, with Mary's children. It was important for me to learn to be as gentle and as fair as possible, so all discussion of the subject was practice.

Normally, the way people might react to my ideas or thoughts was not of great importance to me unless there was a risk of upsetting them. But I felt it was essential to work out how to make contact with the family without upsetting anyone, particularly as these people mattered to me so much. The internal and external discussions were a prelude to facing Mary's children with as much consideration as possible, should I ever be lucky enough to find them.

Now I started to think of how I could introduce myself to them, or if indeed I should do so at all. Losing a parent and the fear of being abandoned rank as the greatest fears a child can have. These people had suffered such a loss in childhood that I might well feel I had no right to cause them any more unease. Yet where did my responsibility lie? Would it be fair to mention reincarnation at the outset, or should I try to let them develop their own feelings about all of this without mentioning mine? Questions that had not bothered me before suddenly seemed very important, and the responsibility felt enormous.

However, my new-found confidence could not be punctured, and it made me feel a closer kinship with others. Consideration of the needs of others seemed even more important, and I knew now that the search for Mary's children could really begin. Somewhere there were people who could answer my questions and lead to answers. A point had been reached where there would be no turning back.

6

Search for My Children

At this point in the search – towards the autumn of 1989 – I assumed that finding out about Mary's family would be a long process. As it happened, this assumption was wrong. From the simple realisation that I was not using all the available resources came success. Since I belonged to Mensa I could contact other members better geographically placed than I was, and they perhaps could find out what I needed to know. So I wrote two letters to members listed as living near to Malahide, and was both surprised and delighted when both answered. One in particular was able to give me the name of the owner of the old building I had seen along Swords Road, a Mr Mahon.

I immediately wrote off to him, asking about the building – whether it had been there for a long time; if it had once been used as a cottage; and whether he remembered a family, who had lived in a cottage in that lane, who had five or more children and whose mother had died in the 1930s. His reply came back fairly swiftly. The building had been erected in the 1930s by his father, *after* the period I was researching.

It had always been used as a barn. He also gave me details of the houses in Swords Road at that point – a mere hamlet, labelled on the map as Gaybrook. (This was obviously why the name seemed so familiar to me, although *inside* I had always known that this was where Mary had lived.) He did not specify whether the house I had asked about was the first on the left, but he did say that this was the only one in the lane with a large number of children, and this was the only family whose mother had died in the 1930s.

Feeling that the jigsaw pieces were beginning to come together, I hastily sent off a second letter in which I communicated a few more details, such as the name Mary. I asked if Mr Mahon knew anything about the husband, and what had happened to the children. If these details matched as well, I realised, the chances that this was my past life family were greatly increased. My main hope, though, was that Mr Mahon could tell me the surname of the family.

As I impatiently waited his reply, Colin Skinner – the theology student based in Dublin – contacted our mutual friend Mr Coulter to report on his progress. He had found the church in Malahide of which I had given him a description and a drawing. Apparently he had recognised it immediately, which delighted me. It was a bit of independent agreement, something that I had hoped for. (I became increasingly glad that I had involved others, even though there had been doubtful names and some confusion at the earlier stages.) However, as expected, Mr Skinner had got no further with research in the church itself, for, as I already knew, St Andrew's was not the one in which records of Mary's family were kept. And, as I was soon to find out, O'Neil was not the family name. This meant that Mr Skinner had been searching for records in the wrong church under the wrong name. Nevertheless, finding the church so substantially similar to a drawing he knew I had done in dreams had rekindled his enthusiasm, and he too had been writing letters of enquiry.

Not long afterwards, I received a second letter from Mr Mahon in Swords Road. To my joy, he was able to remember the names of every family who had lived in that road in the 1920s, and sent me a list. There were a total of nineteen who lived over an area of one mile on the road from Malahide to Swords. He gave details on the family he had mentioned before and these seemed remarkably – and terrifyingly – similar to the name of my memory. Part of his letter read:

Relating to the mother who died in the 1930s – she was Mrs SUTTON. I believe her husband was a British soldier in the 1914–18 war. After her death the children were sent to orphanages – later their eldest daughter MARY returned to the home. I believe the husband returned to the UK to train soldiers, 1939–45. Their children attended the Roman Catholic schools but perhaps their father was a member of the Church of Ireland.

At last I had the name! This seemed to me to be an enormous step forward. The letter also enlightened me about many things that had been puzzling. For instance, I had always felt that Mary's husband was an outsider, and that he had had some involvement in the First World War. As Ireland had been neutral then, just prior to partition, I had wondered whether he had been a volunteer. However, if he were a British soldier that might explain the connection.

That the children were put into orphanages when their mother died was not such good news. I could now appreciate that I had had good reason to worry about their welfare. The letter said 'orphanages' in the plural, which probably meant that they were separated at this traumatic time. Why had their father not kept the family together? Although I had always felt he did not play much part in looking after the children, nor in Mary's thinking about the children's future, I did not believe he could just have stood by and let them be taken away. I did

91

remember that there was a need for the children to be quiet when he returned home from work – he wanted peace after his labours – but surely he would not have let them go?

In some ways I now began to feel worse. If this was the family I was searching for – and the coincidence was so unbelievably huge that I felt I had to accept it probably was – I felt helpless. My whole life had been spent worrying about the children, and the reality was that the concern itself was of no help whatsoever. At the same time there was some element of relief. One of my most constant fears had been for the oldest daughter, whom I now knew was also called Mary. She was so gentle and willing to help that I had been afraid she would have been expected to take over and look after the others. If they had all gone into orphanages, she too would have been looked after, at least for a while until she returned home. It seemed a preferable outcome. The sense of relief, though, seemed to be greater than just concern for her, which I could not understand at all then, and did not fully understand until much later, when the final pieces of the jigsaw were being slotted into place.

I now felt an enormous sense of determination. The strongest element was one of maternal responsibility in that I must now find all the children, despite the fact that nearly sixty years had passed. But there was also a great worry. I did not want to cause any kind of upset to them. I felt protective, yet reaching them with my story might do harm. I wanted to help, not hurt. I wondered if this were possible.

I checked all the details acquired so far with those listed from the memories, to be certain that there really was a match and to confirm its extent. Checking and rechecking were essential. This would continue as each new piece of evidence arrived, because it was important to remain as critical and objective as possible. It would be all too easy to accept a match out of need: it had to be done properly. It would take courage to make an approach even under normal circumstances for genealogical research, but there was no way that these could be deemed normal circumstances.

I wrote back to Mr Mahon, expressing my thanks for his kind help. I also felt it necessary at this point to explain to him exactly what I was trying to do, and why. He might decide he did not want to help any further, but I had no wish to mislead anyone even if telling the truth resulted in making the job harder for me. However, I had another motive. This man obviously knew the family, and seemed to have grown up with the children. It might make it easier for the family to adjust to the idea of me and my memories if there were someone they could talk to about it.

For a change, time seemed almost irrelevant. I reasoned that I had worried for almost thirty-six years – my entire lifetime – and even if it took the patience of a few more years I should not worry. It is strange how sometimes nothing seems to go right and everything is a struggle, and then at other times everything rushes forward. This was a time when things were, for a while at least, rushing forward at breakneck speed.

Having at last got the correct surname, it was time to search through the records again. First I went to the local library, but I was initially thwarted because the Dublin phone book was missing. This meant a trip to the nearest main library, about fifteen miles away – so what should have been a quick dash became a much more lengthy expedition.

This gave me time to think, though. I had intended to look up the surname I now had and list everyone in the Dublin area with a view to writing to them all. But during the drive to the other library I began to calm down from the grip of obsession, and realised that it might be wiser to start by writing to just two or three. So in the comfort of the larger and very well-appointed main library I looked through the telephone book and listed all the Suttons, but chose only three to write to with a similar letter to the one I had sent to the O'Neils.

I also wrote at this time to someone I had not had contact with for nearly a year, the first Mr O'Neil I had chosen at random from the telephone directory and to whom I had spoken on the phone. He had been accepting enough to call me back after looking at the street maps and matching them with my hand-drawn map. I felt he had also been interested enough to merit a further explanation now, plus a resumé of my latest findings. I did not expect him to respond; I just wrote as a matter of courtesy.

A short time later the local history society in Malahide wrote to me. Two people had contacted them with regard to my enquiries about the old building in Swords Road. I was delighted to find that one of them was this same Mr O'Neil. I had half expected him to shrug his shoulders and think it was just that crazy woman again – but he *had* believed me, and believed *in* me. The other was one of the Mensa members to whom I had written.

Old Malahide Historical Society, unaware of the real nature of my enquiry, had gone to quite an effort to find out about the building – but their efforts concerned the barn, not Mary's cottage. They also told me that they were in the process of studying local records in schools and churches, and offered to pass on any information that might be relevant. I replied thanking them for their help and gave further details of the family, including the surname.

Over the course of December, several letters passed backwards and forwards. The three people who shared their surname with my family replied, each saying that they were not related to them. I had hoped that, even with such random picking of three people, I might be lucky: as there were a large number of children there should be grandchildren and great-grandchildren, and I must surely come across *one* relative. However, I was having no success as yet, although I was struck by the geniality and generosity of these people. It was encouraging, particularly in light of the earlier lack of response. Perhaps my letters this last time had been imbued with the confidence in myself and my memories that I had so recently acquired.

One of the three Suttons, a lady from Enniskerry, Co. Wicklow – to the south of Dublin – wrote that she might be able to help in a more positive way. As she had done for some Canadians seeking their families, she could look through papers in the Dublin Records Office. I told her that I had written there myself – with the new name and approximate dates – but that if they were unable to help then I would be happy to accept her kind offer.

Around Christmas she sent a letter saying that the Records Office was only able to provide a limited search, and that, although I said I had rough dates, more precise ones would be needed. The Records Office did indeed write back to tell me that with so little information they could not consider looking for the records requested – and in fact they did not engage in genealogical research anyway. This was irritating because if I had had the information, I would not have needed the records! It was perhaps no great surprise, but it was disappointing.

So, feeling a bit awkward, and saying so in the letter, I enlisted the help of the lady from Enniskerry. The sense of total frustration at not just being able to go to the Records Office myself and spend time on actual physical research was almost beyond endurance.

But then I thought of another potential source. The orphanages where the children were sent might have kept records. So, having once more trawled through the telephone book, I started to write to all the orphanages and children's homes in the Dublin area, asking for any information which could relate to the children. Of course some of these homes might not have existed in the 1930s, and even if they had it was

95

possible that records from so far back might no longer exist. But any chance, however remote, had to be followed up.

I wrote at least fourteen letters, each saying:

Dear Sir,

I am trying to trace a family of children who were sent to Dublin orphanages when their mother died. I realise that a search may require a lot of work and that your records may not even go back that far, but hope that you are able to help. I have written to a number of other orphanages too.

The family name was Sutton. They were from Swords Road, Malahide, and at least six children are believed to have been sent to orphanages. Their mother's name was Mary, and it was after her death in the early 1930s that the family was separated.

Thank you.
Yours faithfully,
Jenny Cockell

My investigations were now running the course of fairly ordinary genealogical research. The family existed – there seemed little doubt about that. All that remained was to find out the children's names so that I could try to trace them, and perhaps Mary's death certificate. These two pieces of information were the minimum needed.

I began to think that I might even be able to handle rejection if I did trace the family. But the thought of not being able to find them at all, and consequently not finding out if they were all right, would be much harder – especially as I had come so far over the last months.

The research had now stretched over several years, and the swing between determined ebullience and nervous anticipation had settled into a repetitive cycle. Waiting for records to be uncovered was nerve-wracking. Even though there had been a number of verified details, I knew I could not begin to feel at ease until there was some definite, documented proof of my family.

The tension caused by the fact that the project was covering somewhat unusual ground made the idea of sharing the experience with a wider audience a way of normalising it. The more this sort of thing could be talked about, the less I would feel I was sticking my neck out. I had kept notes throughout the whole search, and began to feel that, if I could make coherent sense of them, they might be of interest to others in a published form. The possibility of going public gave me something else to think about, and made everything less stressful. It also gave me the chance to consider how best to approach the family.

There were many aspects to take into account. Mary's family should be allowed anonymity if they wished it. I also decided that it was right to contact them if I could do so in a way that allowed them to make up their own minds. Nevertheless, whatever I tried to say when we first made contact would be very difficult.

My greatest hope was to be able to meet face to face: it is easier to look into another person and see the truth in their words, however strange, than it is by letter or even telephone. I was worried not so much about explaining myself but about the difficulties others might have with what I was saying. The family was important to me, and any means of easing the way was worth considering.

I had thought of contacting a priest. Mary was Catholic, and the children had attended the Catholic school, according to Mr Mahon. It seemed appropriate therefore to make some effort to find out what sort of reaction there might be to my experiences. I realised that I sought approval. The part of me that was Mary needed reassurance and my present self needed to know if it were possible to rationalise the phenomenon.

I knew that the obvious view, reincarnation, might not be accepted, but wondered if a broader interpretation might exist. If a priest could accept my story without condemning me, I would feel more secure.

I considered writing a letter for the children, to be included in my account of the story. If I were not able to trace them, then at least they might read it if the story of my search were published. Then I realised that the whole account, which has turned into this book, was written for them and to them. By reading the account itself they would know what the search had meant to me, and what *they* mean to me. After reading it, they would know enough about me to know whether they would want contact. The option should remain theirs anyway.

Another consideration was that going public seemed double-edged. It could help to legitimise the phenomenon, which in turn might make the last stages of my search easier. If I were unable to trace the family in an ordinary way – if they had all moved away, for example – publicity might help me to find them. The down side was that the family might learn about the story indirectly – a sensationalised account, for instance, might reach them before I had a chance to state my views, and could alienate them.

I was burdening myself with endless possibilities, a self-torture of how to cope with this situation or that, long before the need arose. The effect of stress was noticeable in my day-to-day life – odd infections, irritability and tiredness. I knew I was over-reacting, so I tried to calm down, and let things take their course.

During this time replies were coming in from all the orphanages to which I had written. Most reported that they had no family listed with the right name for the right period. But, thankfully, before I could become despondent again the next piece of the puzzle arrived.

On 18 February 1990 I received a letter from a priest in charge of a boys' home in central Dublin. He wrote that the Sutton children were not listed in the records for his orphanage, and that most of the orphanages that had existed in and around Dublin in the 1930s had since closed down, due in part to the modern policy of fostering and adoption. His own boys' home was also closing down, so had I written a few months later I would not even have had this reply. However, he had already made enquiries of the Department of Education (responsible for all admissions to state-controlled orphanages), and of the church in Malahide, and had gained records of baptism for most of Mary's children. He sent copies of these, along with a note, part of which read:

John Sutton and his wife Mary (née Hand) were not natives of Malahide, Co. Dublin, but came to live in the lodge of Gaybrook House, Swords Road. Six children were christened in St Sylvester's Catholic Church, Malahide.

Then the names of six of Mary's children – *my* children – were listed.

1. *Jeffrey (1923)*   married
Sarah O'Reilly

2. *Philomena (1925)*   married Tom Curran

3. *Christopher (1926)*

4. *Francis (1928)*   married
Mary Mulligan

5. *Bridget (1929)*

99

6. *Elizabeth (1932)*   married Thomas
Keegan

The priest's letter offered me great hope and a real opportunity of tracing the family.

7

A Lost Family
is Found

All that time spent racking my brains, and the best I had managed was to run round in circles. But this kind priest had been willing to investigate for me, and now, as a result, I had the names of six of the children, the married names of two of the daughters, and even the names of the wives of two of the sons.

Most importantly, for the very first time I knew that the major name in my quest was right. It was now confirmed that the name of the woman whose life I remember was indeed Mary.

Following this, I went back to the list of Suttons that I had copied from the Dublin telephone directory. I sent the following letters to about twenty people with the right initials in the hope of being able to trace members of the family.

Dear Mr Sutton,
I am trying to trace the children of John and Mary Sutton (née Hand) of Swords Road, Malahide, who were taken into orphanages after the death of their mother in the 1930s.

They are Jeffrey (1923), Philomena (1925), Christopher (1926), Francis (1928), Bridget (1929) and Elizabeth (1932).
I realise that this may not have anything to do with you and must apologise for the intrusion in any case, but if you are part of this family please contact me as it is of great importance to me to find this family.
Thank you.
Yours sincerely,
Jenny Cockell

I then went back to the library and copied out the addresses of all those people with the right surname and initial in the whole of the rest of Ireland. Eventually I wrote to thirty-five more people with the same surname and initials as the sons, and eighteen Keegans, the surname of one of the daughters after marriage. I did realise that only people with a telephone listing could be reached in this way, but I was nevertheless hopeful. Careful records were kept, so that I knew exactly who I had written to and who had replied.

I felt extremely happy. All the doubts and fears, the relentless self-questioning and self-arguing seemed to fade away. I had tried hard to expect nothing because I knew I could not cope with setting my sights too high and then being disappointed. I knew that I had to continue without hoping too much, but at the same time I felt relieved. At last my goal seemed within reach.

I felt I had to write back to the Dublin priest to explain that my knowledge of this family I was trying to trace came from dreams and memories. I did so partly because he specifically asked about my connection, but principally because I felt duty-bound to do so, whatever the consequences. It was not easy to write such a letter, especially as there was so much that I could not properly explain. It was important to me that he should be able to see past the words into the person; for some reason, subconscious and undefined, I felt in need of his support. Or perhaps it was approval that I needed, from someone who might help me to communicate with the children. I was thinking and feeling from two different bases, my own and that of my memory of Mary. From the latter base, I felt I needed to discuss the whole thing with a priest.

The priest's reply, when it eventually came, was wonderful – positive, constructive and considerate. His acceptance of this 'extraordinary phenomenon', in his words, was of considerable value to me. He had done what I hoped was possible: looked at the story without prejudgement and within the framework of his own views. This made me feel much happier about sharing the experience without treading on toes or upsetting people.

And then, on 3 March 1990, I received from the lady in Enniskerry a copy of Mary's death certificate and the birth certificates of two of the children (Jeffrey and Elizabeth), plus dates and details of some of the others. I had rushed her a copy of the list the priest had sent, and luckily she had not started work before receiving it. Without it, her task would have been much longer, although there was already enough information for her to have acquired Mary's death certificate. She had done well to find so many records, and had managed to do the whole lot in one trip.

The records were for the six children who had been christened at St Sylvester's Catholic church in Malahide. There was nothing about the older girl whom I remembered, and whom Mr Mahon had mentioned as being called Mary. Since the oldest boy on the list was only eight in 1932, so I felt there could be more children yet to find. The last child, Elizabeth, had been born on 25 September 1932 and Mary had died a month later, on 24 October, at the age of thirty-five.

The death certificate gave her name as Mary Sutton, of Gaybrook, Malahide, and described her as a labourer's wife. The cause of death was gas gangrene, septic pneumonia and toxaemia. The place where she died was the Rotunda Hospital 'in the District of North City No. 2 in the Union of Dublin in the County of Dublin'. That the hospital was used at least in part for maternity patients among others seemed confirmed by two other pathetic Rotunda entries on the same page – a 'labourer's child' who had died at the age of three days, and a 'plumber's child' who had died at five weeks.

Now at last I had the paper proof I had been looking for. It was odd that the certificates seemed suddenly less important, even though I was extremely grateful to have them. What was primarily on my mind was something far better – a chance to contact Mary's children. That could actually happen quite soon.

Now it was time to look back over the details and see how much had been confirmed. I had got some names wrong, but not much else. The layout of the map had been correct all along, the name Mary was now proved right, and, through naming Gaybrook, the letter from the priest confirmed that the cottage was on the south side of Swords Road. That the cottage was the first building still needed confirming. I had already learned that this house was the home of the only family in the road with five or more children and that the mother had died in the 1930s. Finally the priest's letter had confirmed that the family was not native to Malahide, and that Mary's husband had fought in the First World War.

Under hypnosis, I had named four of the children as James, Mary, Harry and Kathy. James appeared as a second name for Jeffrey, the oldest boy, on the baptismal details I had been sent by the priest. I had suspected that one of the girls was named after her mother, and although she was not on the priest's list of those christened, Mr Mahon in Swords Road did name the oldest girl as Mary when he said that she had come back home after a few years. She must have been one of the children born before the family moved to Malahide; I

Superintendent Registrar's District *Dublin* Registrar's District *North City No. 2*

18 *22*.   DEATHS Registered in the District of ___ *North City No. 2* ___ in the Union of *Dublin.*

In the County of *Dublin.*

No.(1)	Date and Place of Death.(2)	Name and Surname.(3)	Sex.(4)	Condition.(5)	Age last Birthday.(6)	Rank, Profession, or Occupation.(7)	Certified Cause of Death and Duration of Illness.(8)	Signature, Qualification, and Residence of Informant.(9)	When Registered.(10)	Signature of Registrar.(11)
498	18 *22* *Eister* *Twentyfourth Gaytapark Islands Npt Whitehall*	*Mary Sutton*	*F*	*J married*	*35 yr*	*Valourin wife*	*Ja. Sangeven John Freeman Freeman bed*	*John Sutton Cretain Gaytark Whitehall*	*18.. Octr Twenty first*	*G Cresson Registrar.*

Mary's death certificate which I first saw in March 1990.

seemed to remember the actual moving day, when Mary had one or more children in her arms.

I kept trying to picture the children in my mind in case I could pinpoint anything specific that might help them to recognise themselves in my descriptions. The youngest boy ran his hand along the bottom of his jacket, playing with the hem. It seemed to be a nervous habit and might perhaps be retained in adulthood. Could he still be a bit of a loner? The confidence and straightforwardness of the eldest boy were memorable, as were the humour and resilience of the second. I hoped that I remembered enough.

Talking with my mother whilst my daughter was playing with my own childhood baby doll, I realised I had called the doll Elizabeth, the same name as that of Mary's youngest child. I asked my mother if she remembered what I had called the doll, and she did. In fact my daughter too knew that the doll was called Elizabeth. Once more I wondered whether Elizabeth had had the blonde hair and blue eyes of the toy I had cherished so much in childhood.

The details on the death certificate were reasonably consistent with what was expected. I had given Mary's date of birth as around 1898; it was likely to have been 1897, as her age at death was given as thirty-five. She had died in the Rotunda Hospital, which accounted for the feeling of being away from home in those repeated dreams of Mary's death. I remembered white paint and tall windows letting in lots of light. Later I saw photographs of the hospital, which did indeed have tall, elongated windows.

I had often wondered about the reason for Mary's death. There was illness and a prior period of tiredness or ill-health. That could have been the toxaemia, an old name for a number of diseases of pregnancy. There was a fever and difficulty in breathing, which the pneumonia would have been responsible for. Gas gangrene, a form of tissue destruction caused by the soil germ *clostridium*, could have caused great pain as well.

Letters began to arrive in reply to those I had sent in enquiry, but none with any news. Then I wrote a letter to the Dublin *Evening Press* which was published early in 1990. It read:

> *I have been trying to trace a family for a few years without success yet, and have been advised to write to you.*
>
> *My family are the children of John and Mary Sutton of Swords Road, Malahide. On October 24th 1932 Mary died, shortly after the birth of her last child, and the children were placed in orphanages, probably in Dublin.*
>
> *They were Jeffrey James (25/5/24), Philomena (3/8/25), Christopher (15/12/26), Francis (1928), Bridget (1929) and Elizabeth (25/9/32).*
>
> *If possible, I would be grateful for any contact relating to the whereabouts of this family, even if only to know how they are.*

I also wrote to Dr Stevenson, the American who had written about the phenomenon of past lives and who was a leading authority on the subject at the University of Virginia. And, following a BBC documentary about reincarnation – *Many Happy Returns* – I wrote to Dr Fenwick, a psychologist from the London Institute of Psychiatry, who was named in the programme. I hoped that he might be able to put me in touch with someone who could help both myself and the family through what might be a difficult encounter.

I needed to ask for help because I was beginning to panic. I wondered if I had any right to disturb Mary's children or, conversely, if I had the right to keep my story from them. Was I trying to justify myself, or was my need to know about the children's current welfare based on a real and unselfish concern?

Most people's motives are mixed, so I had to accept that some elements that were not in the best interests of others were unavoidable. My worries may seem excessive, but it must never be forgotten that the basis of the feelings involved was maternal protection. The children, though long since grown up and now mostly nearing retirement, were not to be caused any sort of upset.

Of course, there was a chance that I would not have to make any decision – that I might not be able to trace the family at all. For instance, if they had left the country it would be very hard to know where to start.

Shortly after this, interest was expressed in my story by both Dr Stevenson in the USA and Dr Fenwick, who advised me to write to Gitti Coats, a researcher working on a future BBC television documentary series covering various paranormal topics. They could not guarantee that my case would be included in the series, but Gitti and I exchanged detailed letters and had several telephone conversations. She seemed very understanding. However, my feelings about inconsiderate public exposure were still very mixed.

I began to feel tired. It had taken too long just to confirm that the family were real. Now there was still work to be done, there was more waiting, and I could only anticipate more stress.

The Easter weekend brought with it an odd and unexpected experience. Dreams, premonitions or psychic visions can come at any time without warning. Those who are not subject to experiences would probably – and quite reasonably – find it hard to understand how an ordinary dream or daydream could feel so subtly different from one that is psychic. The only way I can describe the phenomenon is that it has a three-dimensional quality, a 'knowing' that it is to do with something happening some*where* or some*when* else.

On this particular occasion, I was a passenger in a car on a longish journey. My mind was drifting in no specific direction, which in retrospect seems to be the ideal state for such experiences. I was running my hand through my hair and was aware that the texture was different. I then noticed that both of my hands were in front of me on my lap, so I realised that the sensation was within my mind rather than of the present. I was aware of the knotty remains of baby hair at the ends of the smooth, straight strands, which would put my age at about two or less. When I looked down I did not see myself at all, but bare feet and slight brown legs. There was a feeling of being an Asian girl, and the sensations were of future and of self. It was very much as though a future self was looking back whilst, in that same slightly absent-minded state, sitting running her fingers through her hair.

The whole thing probably only lasted a minute or two. It was not at all worrying, but very gentle, comfortable and reassuring, even though quite unexpected. Perhaps by accepting the past I was now becoming more able to accept the future. Many might find this revelation too much to accept, but to me it is interesting, because I consider it part of the 'continuation' experience.

From that point onwards I had more experiences of this kind, and a more complete picture began to form. Time is very much linked with the other dimensions and is not static or necessarily consistent. The theory of relativity states that at speeds approaching the speed of light, time slows. At speeds greater than the speed of light the theory is that time would go into reverse.

It then becomes not inconceivable that some element of energy, in this case thought, perhaps covering a brief span of time, might travel fast enough to go back in time and be experienced in the past as though it were a premonition of the future. This could also explain why premonition feels like something that has already happened rather than something that might happen; and why the precise details within a brief one- or two-minute premonition can turn out to be exactly right, yet, being out of context, can cause confusion of interpretation.

*

Despite all my careful and patient work, the first contact with Mary's children came by accident. On 20 April, obviously in response to the newspaper letter, I was sent an anonymous note, postmarked Dublin which contained a scrap of envelope on which was written the name and address of someone who might be one of Mary's children. The name given was Tom Sutton — not a name on the list I had been given, but I wrote anyway. One day not long afterwards, when I returned from work, my husband told me that he had taken a call from a telephone box in Ireland. The caller had told him that they were of the right family, and had rung up straight away out of curiosity.

As I sat waiting for the return call I realised I had no idea what to say. Nearly thirty-seven years of wondering, over two years of searching — and, ironically, I could not think straight.

When the call came, I found myself speaking to the daughter of one of Mary's sons. She told me that Mary had had eight children, and that her father was not Tom but Jeffrey, the second of Mary's sons. He spoke briefly to me himself, and sounded wonderful. He had his own close family, and the daughter who phoned seemed very protective and caring towards her father. It was enough.

The very fact that *eight* children were confirmed reassured me. I had *known* there were more than were named on the Malahide baptismal lists. It was a relief to learn that there were two more children.

I did not explain myself very well, principally to the daughter. For a start it would have been nice to have been able to take more time over the explanation. But, quite reasonably, they were most interested in enquiring about my connection with the family, and my relationship. My reply was not confident or easy, as I was finding the situation much harder than I had thought. I said, 'I know it's going to sound very strange, but I remember the family through dreams.'

This was a simplification of the truth, but I thought it better to go one step at a time. The response was a cautious but gentle 'Oh yes?' To offer reassurance, I described several of the children and mentioned that as a child her father had been rather mischievous, with a terrific sense of humour. She told me that he was still the same. With some surprise in her voice, she was able to confirm descriptions of some of the other brothers, such as the youngest being a loner

Despite an obvious confusion at the other end of the line, I was given various family details and told the addresses and telephone numbers of two of the brothers, Sonny and Francis (Frank). The sons – Sonny, Jeffrey, Christopher and Frank – had all met up a few years before, but the whereabouts of the daughters were unknown. The girls had been sent to a different orphanage, a convent school in fact, and contact had been broken.

I promised to expand on my story as soon as possible, and later sent a copy of the diary that I had kept covering the progress of the last few years. It was full of confusions and the kind of stuff one writes to externalise ideas, but at least it gave the fullest explanation possible. This was preceded by a short letter trying to put forward my motives. I almost expected rejection, as I did not think they would be able to accept any of it.

I was quite sure that Mary's children would think me some kind of lunatic. Just because she and her memories had been with me all my life did not mean that others were going to find that easy to accept. Although the project had occupied my thoughts for so long, the concepts could be quite alien to others.

However, now that I had managed to contact a member of the family, something had changed. I was at last able to accept emotionally that the children had grown up. I had known that they would be in their fifties and sixties, but it took actual contact to release me from that part of the memory that made me feel for them as the children they once were. My feelings remained strongly maternal, but I was able to understand that the 'children' were now self-sufficient. I had been unable to help them in their childhood, yet the whole point behind the memory was the wish to help them, the sense of responsibility I had towards them.

I felt curiously free, but I knew that I had imposed myself on the family in order to gain that freedom from the past. So the sense of being part of the past had changed; the sense of responsibility had changed, but had not completely gone. I was free both to look to the future and to accept the present. . . . But I still felt like their mother.

Answers often bring with them more questions – it is one of the inevitabilities of life. The reality of Mary's family was positive enough, but now I was left wondering where I belonged. The answer would have to be that I belonged in the present. But what of the family I had found? My children? Logic told me to expect nothing. The only way that I could have any part in their lives would be if they wanted it that way. Only time would tell . . .

By this stage I was keeping Gitti Coats, the television researcher, in touch with each step of progress. There seemed to be a reasonable chance that my case would be considered for the projected documentary on past lives. If it were to go ahead, I said, I would want the welfare of the family to be a primary consideration. Gitti impressed me with her attitude: it seemed possible to do this sympathetically. I expect that my slightly neurotic over-protectiveness made the job harder for her, but in the course of the next few months her diplomacy and consideration were very reassuring and of great value to me, as was her involvement in the research itself. It helped that she was able to contribute a methodical and scientific approach to an analysis of the information.

I heard nothing more from Mary's second son or his family. It was what I had expected, but of course I had secretly hoped otherwise. So, having spent time looking at the addresses they had given me, I decided to make a new contact. I chose to get in touch with Sonny, Mary's eldest son, because he lived in England and was within reach if he were willing to see me.

On Tuesday 15 May 1990, I gathered my courage and telephoned. When Sonny answered I heard the soft voice with a strong vestige of a southern Irish accent. Because I had remembered him being very direct and straightforward as a child, I knew that I would have to be very succinct as to who I was and why I was telephoning. This wasn't easy, but I explained that I had remembered the family through dreams, telling him very briefly of the cottage and that it was the first on the left. (Luckily I had already passed on these details to the television researcher.)

This man of seventy-one (he was born in 1919) rapidly assessed the gist of what I was trying to explain. Straight away he confirmed that I was right about the position of the cottage. I was thrilled. This was something I had not been able to confirm until now.

The conversation was easy, much easier than I might have dared to hope. Sonny seemed to have no problem with what must have been a bizarre concept, right out of the blue. There was no indication of rejection, and the questions were relevant and reasonable. Throughout the telephone call, which was not long, I felt as if I were in some kind of trance, yet at the same time there was an intense kind of awareness.

Briefly I was told where the family members were or were thought to be. None of the sisters was in contact with the brothers. Contact between the brothers had only been re-established a few years previously, in the early 1980s, when Christopher, the fifth child, had set out to trace them all after returning to Ireland from Australia. The eldest daughter, Mary, the one I hoped I might find first, had died at the age

113

of twenty-four — in other words, before I was born. As I was told this, I fought off my grief, pushing it to one side to be coped with later.

Mary's son expressed a wish to see me and discuss the memories. I said I would love to, and would arrange a meeting as soon as possible.

After the telephone call I felt indescribably happy. Excitement mingled with relief and every part of life became easier to bear.

The next morning I contacted the television researcher to let her know about this new development. But after consulting her producer, she suggested that they interview Sonny first, before I met him. I felt rather protective and slightly disappointed, but I agreed to her telephoning him to find out how he felt about the idea. When she got back in touch I was told that he seemed quite happy, and a meeting had been arranged for the coming Friday.

This meant that I would have to wait again — something I have always found hard; I was told that it would not be for long this time, though to ensure that the research was conducted properly, I was asked not to make further contact. They wanted to ask Sonny questions and compare his answers to the details that I had already given about his mother and his childhood.

Matters had been taken out of my hands. At the same time I reasoned that it was easier to approach the family in an official way like this, and there was more chance of my being taken seriously. Having rather messed up the initial contact with Jeffrey, the son I had found in Ireland, I told myself that anything that would help cushion the effect was probably worthwhile. There were not very many family members to contact, and I did not want to risk spoiling things.

Not surprisingly, however, I felt a little jealous that on Friday someone else was going to meet Mary's eldest son first. It was not until the following Wednesday, though, that I had some idea of just how long it would be before I too could meet him. Sonny seemed happy about the idea of appearing on camera, so they had to organise a camera crew to be present when we first met. This, we were told, would take a few weeks, during which time there was still to be no contact between us so that details could be analysed properly without our being able to make comparisons. I was asked to remember a few more specific details and to make notes of anything that I might not have included in the material I had already given the researcher.

Letters and telephone calls between Gitti and me went backwards and forwards for about four months. She was also in contact with Sonny while I waited for some definite date or decision. There were times when the frustration caused me to become fractious and probably difficult, but everything was handled carefully. She reassured me by saying that the time was probably of value to Sonny as it could help him think the thing through. And she helped by being considerate in her contacts with him, something that I worried over and bothered her about.

After a number of delays the television company gave me some provisional dates for filming; then, a few days later, Gitti rang and with much apology told me that neither my case nor the other British one was now to be included.

I was assured that it was no reflection on the quality of my case. The decision was due partly to politics, and partly to the fact that the cottage was no longer standing. As television is a visual medium, the lack of pictorial evidence had been a major factor. Surely, the fact that the cottage no longer stood, yet I was happy to describe it, made the case itself stronger?

Sonny and I were both disappointed. But what this did mean was that we were now free to meet. The months from May to September had not been wasted. I telephoned Sonny to ask if I could visit him, and it was arranged for the next weekend. For the rest of that week I willed time to pass – I could not wait to meet the boy, the man, whom I had known in my dreams for so long.

8

Reunions

On 23 September 1990 I visited Mary's eldest son at last. It was a three-hour car journey from home to Leeds, and my family came with me. Despite a stop, we were all a little tired on arrival. I was excited, nervous and visibly shaking.

Sonny's house was in the city outskirts and I had to use a detailed street map to find it amidst the many post-war housing estates. The house itself was set higher than the road, and the obvious effects of a keen gardener showed signs of damage caused by the long hot and dry summer.

Sonny answered the door. He looked a quiet, gentle man, of slightly less than average height and of a slim build that suggested a life of physical activity. He had a warm smile and a gentle manner that instantly put me at ease. We were invited straight in.

Gitti had suggested that the meeting be recorded and I had taken a tape recorder along, but I felt it would be an intrusion to use it. In any case, we just started talking and didn't stop for long enough to think about setting up the machine!

While his wife kindly handed round cups of tea and talked with my husband and children, Mary's son learned more about my dreams and memories that had led me to search for him and his brothers and sisters. And I came to discover just how accurate and detailed those memories were.

It must have been obvious how nervous I was. My conversation was at times stilted, yet Sonny was quite relaxed and, as I soon found, had no problem in talking to people. In subsequent meetings Sonny commented on how nervous I was that day, but at least he understood.

He asked me how I could explain what this memory was. It was very important to me to answer carefully. I said that, for me, it had to be reincarnation, but that this was not the only way of looking at it. I didn't expect everyone to see it in a similar way. He thought about this and seemed happy to leave it at that.

This was a tremendous relief to me. I had been so afraid. Because I had always thought in terms of reincarnation, I saw Mary's children as mine, from the distant past. This was something I did not have any problems with, despite the fact that Sonny was old enough to be my father! As he described his life I felt what can only be described as maternal pride in all that he had achieved. Equally I felt an anguish when he later talked about his worst times.

Gitti had sent us both a list of comparisons she had compiled, since there was no longer any reason to prevent us comparing statements. This gave us an idea of what to expect and what to talk about. It ran to many typed pages, and covered a number of topics which we had both detailed. Now we compared them point for point.

When the document had arrived I spent quite a while looking over it. I was fascinated by the details that were accurate, even some quite small points. I kept showing bits to my husband and saying, 'Look at this!' and 'I got this right too!' and 'Even that very vague memory of the dog was true!' By the time I actually met Sonny that initial excitement had begun to subside a little. We used the list as a starting point for our talk, but mostly the joy for me was in simply being there.

Sonny's reaction to the information on the list was greater than mine. The concept of my 'memories' being so accurate was still new to him. I sat there in a slightly strange state of nervousness, tiredness and caution mingled with relief, while he received each revelation about his childhood with enthusiasm and wonder. How could anyone know so much about his private world?

During most of this my daughter cuddled up to me, not wanting to be excluded. I found her closeness comforting. First we talked about the cottage. It was the lodge or gatehouse to Gaybrook House but sadly neither is still standing. They were demolished in 1959, according to Gitti's research. I had described the cottage as single-storey, brown or buff in colour, but perhaps white. Sonny confirmed that it had, occasionally, been whitewashed. It was not thatched, he told me, and the roof had a pronounced dip in it – a confirmation of my memory. It sat sideways to the road – facing the entrance gate to the mansion, according to Sonny – with a door placed roughly centrally. Each of the two rooms went from front to back and there was indeed a wooden partition just inside the front door, forcing people to turn left or right to go further into the cottage. There was a mention of attached outbuildings. Sonny confirmed all these details.

The gate at the entrance was farm gate-sized and the road had been surfaced at some point. I remembered what must have been the surfacing – large steam rollers, and the smell of tar – and Sonny could remember it too. He added that the gateway was in a semi-circle with three gates, one large and two small.

A stone wall, which I had described as uncomfortable to lean on, ran between the cottage and the lane. I had felt that there might have been stones on edge along the top, which was indeed the case. Similarly we had both described the patch of land beside the cottage which was used for growing vegetables, and the stream running south to north towards the sea, flowing under a bridge on the lane.

I had felt that it was dark when you entered the cottage and knew that there were windows at the front, few if any at the back, and none on the gable ends. Sonny confirmed that the only two windows were on the same side as the front door − two, one for each room, with oval tops that opened.

I had said that the cottage was rented from a man nicknamed Mac, who had work along the coast. It was in fact owned by a family called MacMahon, who also owned Gaybrook House. (As with several of the memories, the feeling about work along the coast may have been part of a separate detail that became confused and tied in at the wrong place. Alternatively Mac may have owned other properties along the coast.)

The position of the wetlands across the road − called the 'Bottoms' by the family, according to Sonny − and the woodlands near the house had been mentioned by both of us. He remembered playing there as a child.

When we discussed Mary's waiting on the jetty, alone and at dusk, Sonny became really animated and showed me a map of Malahide. He pointed out the jetty that I had visited and felt I had recognised as the one from memory. It had once been wooden, as I had described.

'I'll tell you why you remember that jetty,' said Sonny. 'As a boy I used to caddy on the island for the golfers, and at dusk my mother would wait for me on the jetty so that we could walk home together.' He would earn 2s 6d (15p), of which he gave his mother two shillings and kept the sixpence. So I *had* been waiting for a boat, though only a small row-boat ferry. I told him that it had been cold, which I felt through my shawl, and he agreed that it would indeed be cold because of the sea breezes.

We talked about the fields and woods around the lodge. The children would trap pheasants using brown paper sugar bags containing corn, or a flashlight to dazzle them at night. Without this there would have been no meat in their diet. He told me how they also ate raw vegetables taken from the fields and peeled with a penknife. He did have the small black dog that I had described.

The children ran barefoot; their clothes were made out of old garments cut down and remade by their mother. (This was something that I did with my own children, too.) Sonny described his mother as a good needlewoman, something that I had also mentioned.

In the table of comparisons was the description of the trapped hare. I described the position of the snare, adding that it was early morning and that Sonny was about eleven. I talked for a few minutes, and then he just looked at me blankly and said, 'How did you know that?'

I had thought that the hare had still been alive when it was found. Under hypnosis I had said simply: 'It's still alive!' That afternoon Sonny told me that it had been. This was clearly the first piece of information that had really shocked him by its accuracy. The incident was so private to him and his family, how could anyone else know about it?

We talked for a while about food. The main daily meal had consisted of potatoes boiled in their skins, butter and a jug of buttermilk. Sonny started to describe the type of porridge his mother made for breakfast, saying that it was made of pinhead oatmeal. But he did not need to complete the description. I have used pinhead oatmeal myself and know that it makes a thicker, more substantial porridge than with other kinds of oats.

He talked about the range in the fireplace that I had remembered. It had hobs on either side and a hook down the chimney for pots. I felt quite exhilarated – so many of the facts matched my memories exactly!

It was easy to forget that Sonny and I had not shared our past in a normal way. Sitting in Mary's son's comfortable room, talking to him about the years that I felt I had lost, was a traumatic experience, but it made me feel more complete than ever before. The fact that Sonny was so kind and accepting was wonderful. If he had been less considerate and less capable of taking on board such extraordinary revelations, I don't think I could have gone on.

We discussed the people closest to Mary in more detail. The children. My descriptions of them were fairly accurate, though I discovered some were better than others. That the youngest son, Francis, was quiet and fidgeted with his clothing was a feature remembered by Sonny. He showed me a photograph of the brothers taken a few years earlier when they had met up again. In it Christopher reminded me very much, in build and looks, of Mary's father. The strange thing was that he was probably about the same age in the photograph as Mary's father was in my memory.

The pretty little blonde girl whom I remembered turned out to be the seventh child, Bridget. The youngest, the baby Elizabeth, seemed, through Sonny's description, to look very like the doll that I had chosen in childhood and given the same name: she had blue eyes and sandy blonde hair. Could my doll have been a psychological replacement for the baby?

Two babies did not survive. A child between Sonny and Mary died, as well as the son I remembered just before the last child. He was particularly remembered by Sonny. Both Mary and her husband had been told that if she had any more children it would be she who died. Within a year another child was born, which indeed caused Mary's death. Sonny still blamed his father for this.

My description of Mary herself seemed to be accepted. Sonny said she was of average height (hence my feelings when I was thirteen of having grown too tall) and a staunch, sturdy, and happy sort of person. She wore her long, dark hair in a bun. I had repeatedly described Mary's clothes – the blouse with three-quarter sleeves gathered into a narrow cuff, the dark calf-length woollen skirt and shawl. Sonny confirmed all these details. She wore no jewellery, apparently – just a wedding ring.

The memories of the friend who would spend time in the house and talk while Mary worked, and whom I felt went to church with the family, elicited a very positive reaction. She was not called Molly, as I had thought, but Mary Monahan. She also went on those vaguely remembered trips to the city without the children. Those visits were by bus on a Friday night to the market.

At this point I interrupted Sonny and described the market and the street again in great detail. He could not remember if there was a letterbox where I said, and I had not remembered the tram lines, but the rest was the same – cobbled streets and stalls. This was a relief. I had been trying to place this market in Malahide, but could not get it to fit; now I understood. Sonny told me it was Moore Street in Dublin, and that it was very close to the Rotunda Hospital. Sonny and Mary Monahan's son would come to meet their bus when it returned, and the two boys would walk their mothers home.

The memory of Mary's father has always brought with it tremendous feelings of warmth and affection. I had remembered him dressed in scruffy clothes and tending fields. I had been uncertain of his work, and Sonny said that he was the station-master at Portmarnock, a village south-east of Malahide. He lived in the station house. Although I had memories of watching steam trains but not of travelling on them, I had failed to make the connection. It all made a lot more sense when I was told that Portmarnock was a through station where trains did not generally stop. His job was to keep the station clean and to tend the fields that were part of the railway property. He wore not a uniform, but corduroy trousers tied at the ankles with string. He was a

Yorkshireman employed through the British owners of the railway. He had a real sense of humour, which was also remembered by Sonny.

I had described Mary's parents' house as being of stone and standing alone, and of course station houses usually do stand alone. The name of the road I had given as Walldown Lane: it was in fact called Watery Lane (at least I had got the initial right!). Mary and her husband had lived there for a time after their marriage before moving first to Kinsaley, two miles from Malahide, then ultimately to Gaybrook Lodge. Was this perhaps where the Lett family had lived, in or near Portmarnock?

Mary's two brothers whom I had remembered and whom went abroad were Michael and Christopher. Michael went to England, to Kettering in Northamptonshire, while Christopher died during the First World War at Lucknow in India, at the age of nineteen. It was his picture, dressed in the soldier's uniform, that I had vaguely mentioned as being on the wall of the cottage. The picture was quite large and surrounded by a horseshoe-shaped listing of battles. Another photograph in that cottage, that I had not remembered, was that of Mary herself, her hair in a bun.

Apparently Mary had a sister as well, although I had not remembered her. She had four children, and lived in Malahide, on The Hill, the extension of Church Road. Sonny talked about going to visit her there, which clarified yet another of the puzzles. To get to and from The Hill, Mary would have had to walk past both the butcher's shop and St Andrew's church, the one I had described so clearly and had drawn from my memories. I had wondered where Mary had been going, and at last I knew.

My memories of the husband had always been poor. I could remember him as a young man, smart and good-looking, but a bit vain and slightly arrogant. The touch of self-interest at that age tended to make him seem perhaps more attractive to the young and slightly naïve Mary. Certainly I remember the feeling that he was attractive. But later he was seldom there and the feelings altered. I felt that he saw the children as rivals for Mary's attention, and the few words that passed seemed short and gruff. I remembered him as a soldier in the First World War, and then later working with large timbers high up on roofs. I saw a hard-working man of average height, strong with broad shoulders.

Mary's husband's job, at which Sonny and I both agreed he was very skilled, was a scaffolder. He worked with pride, using huge poles secured with wire ropes – thus the remembered roof work, the large timbers and the smell of sawdust. He was called John Sutton and had been a soldier, but he was not British. He was from Co. Kildare, and during the First World War had been in the Royal Dublin Fusiliers. Sonny agreed that he was a very smart-looking man, of average height, very fit and lean, and said he had black hair going grey down the sides.

Sonny told me his father had been violent both to the children and to his wife, hitting her and beating them with a large, brass-buckled belt. He had been a drunkard for as long as Sonny could remember, spending most of his free time in the pub. If Mary wanted to be certain of any housekeeping money at the end of the week, she had to get it from him while he was still sober and before he spent it all.

This revelation made me understand so many things – it explained the over-riding sense of responsibility for the children, which I could never truly comprehend, the sense of quiet caution, the occasional fear. As Mary, I had no recollection of the violence, but similarly, in my own life, I have virtually no recollection of my father's violence. In both cases I have been told about it, and I remember the fear but little else. I believe, and it is commonly acknowledged, that when people have an accident or something equally traumatic happens to them they tend to blank out the worst part of the experience. Abuse, whether physical or mental, is damaging to one's sense of self-worth, and to remember it with any clarity makes sufferers so fearful of life that it becomes almost impossible to continue. One either lives in constant fear and without any self-respect, or one pushes the events as far away as possible in order to carry on. This was, in a sense, what I had been doing throughout my life because of what I had suffered in childhood. When I realised that, as Mary, I had been carrying the same sort of repressed horror, I did not wonder any more at the problems that had dominated my life.

As Mary I remember fear, but not why I felt afraid. I remember that Mary's husband was not there for long stretches of time, and yet I had to wait and be ready for his return. I remember a sense of having to do things properly, but not the punishment that would follow if I did not. The main emotion was always a huge need to protect and be responsible for the children.

Thinking about John Sutton, Mary's husband, I began to feel almost sorry for him, rather than angry. If he had been the sort of person who was able to talk about his feelings, if he had not had to work such long hours, if there had not been so many children, might he not have been a different man? After Mary died he had stayed on in the lodge for a few years, then married again and went to Scotland in either late 1939 or early 1940. Not surprisingly, that made me feel very angry, particularly when Sonny continued with his story of what had happened to the children.

The best thing about meeting Sonny, apart from getting to know a lovely person, was finding out at last what had happened to the family after Mary's death. The news about them was by no means good, but at least I now knew.

The baby Elizabeth had been taken away by her paternal uncle while the father was out. Sonny had handed her over,

126

and was later severely scolded by his father for doing so. Yet he was only a boy, trying to do what he was told by his uncle. He could not have looked after a baby at the age of thirteen; neither could his father, who was at work all day. His father went to his brother's house in Leixlip, Co. Kildare, to get the baby back. They refused to return her. He eventually accepted defeat, and the girl was adopted by the brother's family. Sonny was not invited to visit, so did not see her again.

The other children, except for Sonny, were taken from their father by the authorities as he was deemed unfit to look after them. The three boys were placed in the Artane Industrial School, a Christian Brothers' orphanage in Dublin. They ran away from there a year later, and were resettled in an institution in Cork. Unable to travel that far, Sonny lost contact with them for nearly fifty years. The three other girls were sent to a convent school in Booterstown, Dublin, so Sonny was able to visit them from time to time. However much they might have hated it, I could not help feeling they were better off than they would have been at home.

For Sonny, though, who *was* still at home, things got a lot worse. His father must have felt quite broken and became even more violent.

At seventeen Sonny lied about his age and enrolled in the Free State Army. From there he had married, gone to England and joined the RAF. His first wife had died, but he had later remarried very happily.

With Sonny away, Mary, the eldest girl, had been taken out of the orphanage and sent home to look after her father. Having heard how hard life had been for Sonny during those years alone with his father, enduring beatings and the constant aggression, I could only guess at what happened to his sister. Eventually she escaped too. She was lucky to find a very considerate and loving husband. It was a tragedy that she died so soon after, in childbirth.

Philomena and Bridget were much younger than Sonny, so while he was away in the Army they were still at the convent and he saw little of them. Before he left Dublin for good, though, he saw two of his sisters married and with children. Philomena had eight, and Bridget two.

For a week or so after visiting Mary's son I was so happy that several things did not immediately sink into place. I didn't see all the implications of our meeting. My own childhood was sufficiently unpleasant that I now find it difficult or painful to try to remember it. I was thirteen when my parents separated and, although life was a struggle, my mother managed. She was able to find somewhere for us to live, enough money to feed us, and eventually provide a better, if leaner, life. Sonny was thirteen when his mother died. His home life had always been bad, with a drunken father who beat his wife and children, but after his mother's death it became unbelievably worse.

I had caused someone whom I so desperately wanted to find, whose well-being was so vitally important to me, to remember and relive the worst moments of his life. But Sonny seemed to accept me and we wrote to each other frequently. I for my part was trying to say things I had not managed to express at our meeting, while he once again described his childhood after his mother's death. This poignant letter was actually one he had sent to Gitti:

After my mother died in 1932 my life as a thirteen-year-old was in a turmoil, the bottom had fallen out of my life. . . . She had been wrapped up with her children, but at the same time she had to put up with the beatings and black eyes. Many a time as a boy I stepped between them and then my drunken father would beat me for interfering. It was worse when he came home drunk from the pub with cuts all over his face through fighting with his mates. He would take his revenge out on my mother and us children. None of us were safe when he had a drink.

Further in the letter he describes the sort of food they had to manage on.

Our main meal was potatoes boiled in their jackets with buttermilk and some butter she would scrounge from the farmer. Most of our food we had at night. When it was dark we would go into the fields and steal potatoes, cabbage and turnips so our mother could feed us. Many and many a time she got no money off my dad as he spent it all in the pub.

Some of us children would work in the fields for a few pence, the others would go into the woods and cut branches off trees and cut them into logs for our mother so she could have a fire and do her baking. But if we did not and my father's meal was not ready my mother and us children got a sound beating.

She was only a young woman but she looked like an old woman, the life was drained out of her with childbirth and the beatings she got.

On a subsequent visit I found that, to my relief, although remembering his childhood had caused Sonny to go through a number of painful experiences, the net effect was one of getting things off his chest. It had had a positive rather than negative result.

Sonny later sent me another letter, again about the years after Mary died.

I was only thirteen years old. I had to go to school and work in the fields and look after the home from the time I got home from school. I had to have his meal ready at whatever time he came home, if not I got a beating.

129

I left school at fourteen and went to work for a farmer . . . in Yellow Walls. My day started at 4 o'clock in the morning.

His work was filling two horse-drawn carts with vegetables, such as cabbage and potatoes, and with straw or hay. He would then walk the carts nine miles to the markets in Dublin and could be there until 6.30 or 7 p.m. or when the load was sold. Then he might have to deliver some of the goods to other parts of the city before going back to a yard in Dublin and loading with manure for the return journey. He would then walk the nine miles back to Malahide. When he had brought the vegetable carts back he would have a meal in the farmer's house and then unload and load the carts for the next day. By this time it was late. He was paid less than a pound a week, but never in cash. 'The farmer also had a shop,' he wrote, 'so instead of getting paid in money I used to draw my wage in such as cigs for my father, bread, tea, sugar.'

If he stayed at home he was expected to keep house for his father as his mother had done, and he took the brunt of his father's aggression. He says, 'I have had more black eyes and bruises than a boxer.' He often went hungry, and neighbours started to feed him.

I put up with the treatment for a year. So I started sleeping out at night in hay barns and ditches, anywhere I could get shelter for the night. And he would be out looking for me. He found me a few times and up to this day I won't forget the beatings I got. My friends and neighbours would not give me a night's shelter for when he found out he would be to their homes making trouble for them. At times he would have the police looking for me. I put up with that life for four years, just.

Joining the Army under age was probably the best thing he could have done, because after that he was free of his father.

Each time Sonny and I meet more things crop up in connection with the memories, or with my own behavioural aspects, that tie in with the past. Sonny told me that his parents argued, which at first sounded like a two-way thing. I was about to disagree when he qualified what he had said. Apparently it was all one-sided, as Mary did not dare contradict her husband or stand up for herself. That seemed to fit in with the way I remembered things. It tied in, too, with the way I myself am, particularly as I was in childhood and early adulthood. If anyone raised their voice to me or was particularly dogmatic, I would rather walk away than stand my ground. It is only over recent years that I have discovered it is sometimes possible to put a point of view gently, even when other people's voices are raised, without fear of reprisal.

Other details have begun to fall into place, too. I have always been unsure whether the husband went to church with the family. Apparently he was a Catholic and accompanied them to the church, but never went inside; this was possibly what had caused the confusion.

The garage on the corner of Swords Road that I had not recognised on my visit to Malahide was mentioned by Sonny. Through discussion we realised that it had been built a few years after a fire in a building close to the corner. The fire was in 1926. In other words, the garage was built at about the time of Mary's death or even afterwards.

I had thought that the kitchen area was on the side of the cottage near to the road, taking up the whole building front to back, and this was indeed the case. There were only two rooms anyway. The children all slept in two beds in the bedroom; the kitchen was where Mary and her husband slept, though with only two rooms the use of the word 'kitchen' falls short of describing the function of the room.

With my passion for Irish folk music, especially performed live, I was not surprised to learn that the only real family outings were two or three trips a year to Crossroads, on

Yellow Walls, where there was dancing to a traditional group. This was surely the occasional trip in the opposite direction to Malahide centre that I had remembered and mentioned.

Sonny told me of a builder's yard in Malahide which belonged to someone related to Mary's sister's husband. When we had sorted out the position – on The Mall, almost opposite the end of Church Road – I said it was no longer there. Then I asked about the large wooden gates that were somehow so significant in my memory. The builder's yard had a pair of large wooden gates, said Sonny, and another puzzle was answered.

I had described flat round bread and this turned out to be traditional Irish soda bread. And when Sonny said that he preferred the bread that was made in the large pan I was able to describe how it used to rise out of the top of the pan when it was cooked.

Each and every time I see Sonny, speak to him, or get a letter from him, yet more pieces are added to the jigsaw, and my picture becomes more complete.

Sonny encouraged me to get in touch with both Frank and Christopher to let them know what was going on. He was very keen that things should be handled fairly, and wanted me to make this contact. I wrote to both, but neither responded. However, as a direct result of my letters both of them started to write to Sonny again. At least this was positive, and I was satisfied that my maternal instincts had served to rekindle family feeling.

Then, in October 1990, through an advertisement that I had placed in the Dublin *Evening Press*, I heard from the youngest of Mary's children, Elizabeth, the girl who had been adopted. I was overjoyed. Now Betty Keegan from Rathfarnham, she was sixty and married with six children. She had not been told until she was sixteen or seventeen that she was adopted, and that she had brothers and sisters; by then she had no way of knowing where the rest of the family were. She had always wanted to find her relatives, and the ad in the paper had seemed heaven-sent. Her letter, though, was reserved and cautious, belying her true feelings of excitement, which were expressed later.

Because I now knew what had happened to the children, and had had such a good response from Sonny, I felt no immediate need to explain to Betty the reason for my involvement. It was more important to give her a chance to find out about her own family without my getting in the way, or adding an unnecessary complexity. I put Sonny and her in touch with each other, and also gave her addresses for the other three brothers in case she wanted to contact them.

Another reason for my reticence was that of the four brothers with whom I had made contact, only Sonny had wanted to talk to me. Jeffrey had never been in touch again, and Christopher was happier to ask his brother about things than to contact me direct. But as it turned out, I was accepted by more members of the family as time went by.

I had written to Frank again in October to let him now I had managed to trace his sister Betty. It was not until the end of December that his daughters wrote back to me, apologising about the time taken to reply. They explained that their father was very dubious and did not believe in reincarnation. They themselves were interested, however, and wanted to know more about their grandmother and their family history. Could I fill them in? A slow but steady exchange of letters followed.

To have such contact with an increasing number of Mary's family was a great relief to me, and I felt incredibly happy. But there were some necessary adjustments in my own life that I had not anticipated.

It had not occurred to me that my two children would feel threatened by my discovery of Mary's children, as I had such a close and trusting relationship with them. But my daughter went through a very uncomfortable phase when she realised that Sonny, in particular, was going to remain part of my life. Suffering from what I can only describe as sibling rivalry, she needed a great deal of reassurance that she was special in my life and would remain so. The discussion had to be handled extremely carefully. I could not lessen my feelings for Mary's children in her eyes, or she might feel that she would become less important to me in time or with age. Yet she needed to know that the way I felt for her was extra special. Eventually we hit upon an acceptable formula. She was special, all children were special to their mothers, and my feelings for Mary's children were also special – but different, because I was different now. The jealously slowly subsided as we spent time discussing the situation over and over again until she felt secure once more.

My son did not react in the same way, but I could not help comparing him with Sonny at a similar age. They are very different people, but some of the feelings and similarities demand comparison. I see the same sense of independence and responsibility, the same open but realistic approach to life, enhanced by a gentleness and consideration that mark a man above others. It is with great joy that I look forward to a future that I feel was taken away from me once before; watching my children grow into adults.

Whilst searching for my other family I had compiled a large and heavy file of letters and information. I had kept the bill from the hotel in Malahide, my air travel details and every letter from that point on. I had maps acquired from 1980 onwards, as well as dozens of letters from children's homes and people with the same surname as Mary and the children, and who might have been related. The most important letters were from Mr Mahon in Swords Road and the Dublin priest who had been so kind. I also had Mary's death certificate, and birth certificates for Jeffrey and Elizabeth and all the communications with the television researcher.

There were two reasons why I needed such a complete dossier. It represented my proof, a record of all communications and discoveries which others might check if necessary for details, and dates and so on. But mainly it was my compensation for time missed while the children grew up. All mothers keep mementoes of their children's lives, and so my files were a kind of reassurance, something to help me feel involved and part of the family. Reading through all the letters again helped me to accept that I did not have to worry any more or feel so tormented and responsible.

By March 1992, the collection of letters had grown considerably as the number of family members in touch with me had slowly increased. I also had a family tree and many photographs. I wanted to know anything that the family might want to tell me. There was so much to catch up on. Sonny had eight children – four sons and four daughters, the youngest of whom I met on my second visit and found to be a friendly, gentle lady of my own age. Each time we meet I hear more about his children as well as his own life. One of the most recent discoveries, for instance, is that he was born in England. His parents spent a short while with Mary's brother Michael in Kettering immediately after their marriage, before returning to Ireland and to Mary's parent's house in Portmarnock.

The second child was Mary, the daughter who shared her mother's name. She was born in 1922 and died at the age of twenty-four. All I have in my file for her is a search document from the Records Office, showing they were unable to trace her birth – certainly before the move to Malahide, perhaps in Portmarnock? – and a photocopy of a photograph that her husband kept with him all his life until he too died at Christmas 1991. He lived near Sonny, and had kept up contact and friendship over the years. He very kindly allowed me to borrow the photograph and make copies for myself and Sonny. I also sent him an enlargement, as the original was a small group photograph, and all by return post so that he was not parted from the cherished memento for too long.

I had photographs of Jeffrey, the second son, which were given to me by Sonny. They had been taken a few years previously, on the occasion when the sons had all got together again. This was the son I had first contacted but from whom I had received no further response. Also in my file were the cutting of my letter to the Dublin newspaper, looking for the family, and the piece of torn envelope with the right address but the wrong first name, sent to me anonymously.

The fourth child, Philomena, who was born on 3 August 1925, was last known to lived in Dolphins Barn road in Dublin, but that was in 1955. Her husband worked on the golf links at Velvet Strand, Portmarnock. I tried churches in the area, but to no avail. Sonny believed that she might have gone to London, so once again I placed adverts in London papers and telephoned everyone in the London phone book with her married surname. Eventually I employed the services of the Salvation Army, but without success.

Christopher, the son born in 1926, still hoped to visit his brother Sonny – they had not seen each other since that reunion – but had had to postpone repeatedly due to ill-health. I have been invited to meet him but have not yet been in direct contact. Replies still seem to go via Sonny. It was he who had managed to trace his brothers and get them together again.

The youngest son, Frank, born in 1928, made my day by speaking to me on the telephone at Christmas 1991. I had been in touch with his daughters for about a year, and they had sent me his birth certificate to photocopy and return. This to me indicated an unusual level of trust.

The next child, the seventh, Bridget or Bridie, the one I remember as sweet-natured, pretty and blonde, has still not been traced. She was born in 1929 and as an adult lived in Rathmines, Dublin. Her husband was in the Air Force. Bridget too is believed to have gone to London in the 1950s, but the Salvation Army could not find her.

The eighth surviving child, Elizabeth or Betty, the girl who was born in October 1932 just a few weeks before Mary's death, had not yet been in direct contact with me. However, I did eventually explain my connection to her, about a year after she first responded to the newspaper letter. I have one brief letter in my file for her, which was her initial reply, a copy of her birth certificate, and a colour copy of a photograph sent to Sonny which he then lent to me. He knows how important to me all these little things are. Sonny has been my lifeline and encouragement throughout.

From each of the family members I'm in contact with I gain news about children and grandchildren, and I delight in each snippet, extremely grateful for the level of acceptance and friendship offered. I feel very lucky.

In 1992 Sonny decided that he wanted to visit his family in Ireland. He made arrangements to go in July, and asked me if I could organise some sort of newspaper coverage – after all, he was going to see Betty for the first time in some sixty years! I duly wrote to the *Irish Independent* and, when Sonny met Betty on 24 July 1992, the paper published a short account of their story and a very brief mention of the fact that it was my research that had brought them together. Sonny also managed to visit both Christopher and Frank, although he was unable to see Jeffrey. I was only sad that I could not be there myself.

Geraldine Collins' piece in the *Irish Independent* about the reunion was followed up by a story by Steven McGrath mentioning the reasons behind my research. It was Frank who had instigated this, and as far as I was concerned this was wonderful. It encouraged a lot of interest and perhaps would help trace Philomena and Bridget and promote more trust from the children. After the article was published I received a lovely letter from Betty. She had been perhaps reassured by Sonny that I was not entirely strange or un-approachable.

However, the best thing that happened was the finding of Philomena, or Phyllis, as she was now known. After all my investigations in England, she had in fact been living in Ireland. Her son read the piece about Sonny and Betty in the paper and thought it must be about his mother's family. She contacted the newspaper and was given the addresses of her siblings. The *Irish Independent* even wrote to me, which I thought was extremely kind of them.

Even though I had managed to trace so many of the family, I found that I was still having dreams and daydreams recalling small facets of Mary's life. I had come full circle and maybe I could now allow myself to accept everything as I had done in childhood.

One such detail was of waiting outside the local school with lunches for the children. The children would come out to collect their food and drink and return to the school building fairly soon. It was after meeting Phyllis on 4 October 1992 that this was confirmed by her. She told me that she remembered her mother bringing tea and sandwiches to the school gate for lunch. She also spoke about the short-cut by the side of the Protestant church, which I had tried to find and use whilst in Malahide. I told her that they had built a house in the field now, and that I didn't think it was possible to get across any more. And, as some of my earliest memories were of asking the oldest daughter, Mary, to fetch water, the description that I was then given of the sister's going to the water pump was of value in reassuring me of another small detail.

The meeting with Phyllis – at Sonny's house – gave me great pleasure, as well as some relief. She was only the second of the children that I had actually met. Probably the highlight was that Phyllis had the only known surviving photograph of Mary. She had kindly provided copies for each member of the family, and one for me.

The photograph was of Phyllis at the age of about two, with her mother. Mary would have been about thirty-one at the time the photograph was taken. It was something that I had wanted and needed. To be able to look at a photograph to see the physical evidence, to fill in that piece of the jigsaw, to be certain. I couldn't stop looking at the picture. I have framed my copy, and placed it where I can see it when I wake each day.

It was inevitable that I searched her face for comparisons. Was she what I had expected? Was she as I had described her? Indeed she was. I looked for comparisons with myself and felt that there were postural and expressional similarities. There could have been a family relationship, even though I knew that there was not.

The discussion at that meeting was most constructive. Phyllis had had the least time to adjust to the phenomenon of my involvement, and had talked with friends to gain insights into it. I myself found throughout the search that this was necessary. A priest had suggested to her that reincarnation was not tenable, but had been able to put forward a view that seemed more easily acceptable to her. This was that Mary spoke through me to reunite the family.

Obviously this is now how I see the phenomenon, but neither is it my place to insist on my own view – that I feel that I was Mary in a previous life – being accepted. It has been sufficient just to be accepted by the family in any way that they are willing to accept me.

Things, as a result, are much better. It feels as though I have passed through a barrier and have done so not alone but with the help of my husband, children and mother, close friends and, of course, Mary's children and grandchildren. I realise that, whoever I was, I am myself now and have this life to live. But if I can do that and still hang on to Mary's family, still keep contact and be allowed to feel in some small way involved, I will feel rewarded, complete. Each time I look into my heavy file with its photographs and letters, I delight in the family and the individuals who have bothered to take the time to listen to what I was saying and not dismiss me. I still stay slightly back, not pushing my way forward, for fear of causing offence. I will probably always hold back a little – it is an integral part of my nature. I still find it hard to believe that the search is almost over. Almost? There is one person yet to find, Bridget. Perhaps she will be found, perhaps not. At this point, at least I feel willing to accept that whatever will happen must be accepted.

For as long as I can remember Mary has been a part of me. The worry about the children sometimes in the background, sometimes in the foreground, was always there. Now, at the age of thirty-nine, I have found most of these children and know what happened. If none had been willing to listen to me I could not have found anything out. By his acceptance Sonny has given me what I have searched for. The sense of responsibility and guilt have fallen away, and I feel a sense of peace that I have never really known before.

Postscript

During the weeks immediately before visiting Malahide in 1989, I dreamed several times of going to the site of the cottage and finding just the foundations and some stonework. In this dream I was with other people and was searching with them for the remains that I knew were there. Visiting Malahide then, I was alone and I did not find the ruins. But in 1992 Sonny visited the site with his wife, sister and some of her family, and did find the remains. They were exactly as they had been in that dream.

It was as though I was being told not to look for an existing cottage, but I felt also that I was yet to revisit the area with others and to live out that dream. And indeed, in February 1993, after I had finished this whole account, I did visit Malahide again.

Early that spring, in discussion with my publishers, it was decided that it would be useful if I could return to Ireland for a day to take photographs and perhaps see some of the places I had been unable to visit on my previous trip. The camera I had taken with me then had been faulty, so I had come home with only a few usable pictures.

On this occasion I would be driven from place to place and it would be possible to visit Portmarnock, where Mary grew up, and Kinsaley, the village in which Mary had lived before Malahide, and where, I had been told, we might find her grave. The list of places to visit went as follows:

In Malahide:
The cottage or lodge remains.
The remains of the stone supports of the gateway to Gaybrook House and the lodge, which I had seen but had been confused by.
St Sylvester's Roman Catholic church.
St Andrew's church, Church Road.
The butcher's shop in Church Road.
The jetty.

In Portmarnock:
The station-master's house where Mary grew up.
The farmhouse belonging to the Lett family, where Mary worked before marriage.

In Kinsaley:
The church and graveyard where I was told Mary had been buried.

In Dublin:
Moore Street, where the Friday market had been.
The Rotunda Hospital, where Mary had died.

It was with great sadness that I learned, a few days before the trip, that Mary's second son had died. (He is the only one of the children for whom I have not used a real first name, but instead called him Jeffrey.) Sonny phoned me to let me know. Jeffrey had been the first of Mary's children to contact me and speak with me, and I felt a sense of grief.

At Dublin Airport I was met by Genny, the Irish representative for Piatkus Books, and we drove straight to Malahide. This, apparently, was where Genny had spent her childhood holidays, and it evoked pleasant memories for her.

Driving along Swords Road towards the site of Gaybrook, it was obvious that a great deal had changed even in the few years since my first visit. We parked in a housing estate which had not been there in 1989, and walked towards Malahide looking for the remains of the gateway. There was a sudden moment of absolute horror when I realised that a large area of the south side of Swords Road at that point had been levelled. Earth-moving machines had ripped at the topsoil, trees had been uprooted and markers were placed for new houses. I kept saying, 'I think it's gone', but then, right at the edge of the site, I saw the piers of the gateway. They seemed more damaged than before, but I was much more certain now that this was the right spot. In many ways the clearing of the land had made the area more accessible. There was less there to cause confusion, so it was easier to focus on the right place.

A small section of stone wall with its topping of stones set on edge remained, and this butted up to one of the remaining piers. To the right, the trickle that was left of the stream had been confined within a concrete conduit. The area of wild and unkempt land, covered with trees and brushwood, was now limited to a very small section just behind this little remnant of stone wall. Standing by the wall, I realised that through a mass of brambles I was looking at the gable end of the lodge, my cottage.

I tried to approach it by entering through the old gateway and walking towards where the door had once been. This turned out to be impossible because of the bushes and brambles. After several attempts I went back to the road and scrambled over the wall to try to reach the cottage from the rear. The outbuilding which had been attached to the back of the main room, or kitchen, had a wall around it that was now only about waist height. This negotiated, I found myself standing inside the shell of the cottage.

For a moment or two I stood, aware of both the past and the present simultaneously. The ruins of that tiny cottage sharpened the focus of my memory and I could picture the internal walls, the fire for cooking on, and other parts that were now gone. Memories flooded back and the physical remains added an extra dimension, making it so very easy to recall. I knew that all I needed was to have the chance to be there, to remember that place in a special way, and then to say goodbye. It seemed that time had caught up with my cottage but had allowed it to remain neglected and untouched long enough for me to be able to find it. Now the bulldozers were about to move in.

Genny climbed over the wall and we stood outside, in what used to be the garden. The area where potatoes had once grown was now filled with scrub and bushes. A few large trees grew where the edge of the vegetable patch had been, and beyond those trees lay open fields. I told Genny of the woodland that used to be there, and of the meadow by the lodge. I was aware of the changes, yet delighted at the chance to look at this small patch of land again, this time through my own eyes, as this self, not as Mary, not as a memory.

We walked around Malahide and I saw again those landmarks that were so familiar. We walked by St Andrew's church, which had been passed on the visits to Mary's sister, and the butcher's shop and out to the jetty. Genny remembered that the jetty had been wooden during her own childhood, too.

Back in the centre of the village we entered St Sylvester's church. I felt only that it was too quiet without people. On a Tuesday morning such as this it was empty, but my only memory of it was of people gathered there and talking on the way in. It had been as much a social occasion as a religious one in my memory.

We found the church in Kinsaley but were unable to find Mary's grave. Over the course of the day we tried several graveyards – but without luck. I later found that the old graveyard at Kinsaley was the right one, but that the grave, on the left-hand corner by the road, was unmarked.

At Portmarnock we found the railway, but the old station house where Mary had grown up was no longer standing. A man there, whose son worked for the railway, said that there had once been a house, but could offer no further help.

We drove around Dublin and found a church named by Sonny, where we thought Mary had married. (This later turned out to be the wrong church.) Then we went on to find Moore Street and the Rotunda Hospital, driving through the busy city in bright sunshine. The hospital was pretty much as I had expected it to be and, although there were a number of impermanent-looking buildings at the back it was relatively unchanged from memory and the old postcard that I had found a couple of years previously.

At the main registry of births, deaths and marriages in Lombard Street we found Mary's marriage details. So now we had a date and the name of the church where Mary had married. The date was 22 July 1917, and it had been witnessed by Mary's brother and sister. This was the younger of her two brothers, who soon afterwards died.

The districts of Portmarnock, Kinsaley and Baldoyle were part of the same parish, so it was at the Baldoyle church that Mary married. We visited the church and I later learned from someone there that Mary's date of birth was 1 December 1895.

A great deal had changed. Places that had been small villages were now quite busy. Many buildings that might have been standing during the 1920s or earlier were no longer there:

First Page.　　　Superintendent Registrar's District of _North Dublin_

19<u>17</u>. Marriage solemnized at the Roman Catholic _Church_ of _Baldoyle_ in the Registrar's District of _Baldoyle_
in the Union of _North Dublin_ in the County of _Dublin_

Marriage No. _5_

Registered by me, this _31st_ day of _July_ 19<u>17</u>.

Moore Deputy Registrar.

No. (1)	When Married (2)	Name and Surname (3)	Age (4)	Condition (5)	Rank or Profession (6)	Residence at the Time of Marriage (7)	Father's Name and Surname (8)	Rank or Profession of Father (9)
58	July 22 1917	John Sutton	full	Bachelor	Soldier 76th R.D.F. Regt	Portmarnock C/o Dublin	Michl Sutton	Labourer
		Mary Hand	full	Spinster	—	Portmarnock C/o Dublin	John Hand	Labourer

Married in the Roman Catholic _Church_ of _Baldoyle_ according to the Rites and Ceremonies of the Roman Catholic Church by me, _R. Cornick P.P._

| This Marriage was solemnized between us, | { John Sutton
{ Mary Hand | in the Presence of us, | { Christopher Hand.
{ Bridget Hand |

Mary's marriage certificate found at the main registry in Dublin in February 1993.

some cleared for housing developments, a few others just left to fall down. The original station house at Portmarnock was probably not very large; my memory is of a fairly small house. And the farmhouse where I believed Mary had worked could have gone, or could have become almost impossible to find. But even without finding everything the day had been extremely productive.

For me, perhaps the very best part of the day was meeting three of Mary's children at the airport before I left. Now, meeting Frank and Betty for the first time, and Phyllis for only the second, I was profoundly aware of how lucky I had been since my first nervous phone call to Sonny. I had not expected anyone to want to listen, but Sonny had listened and he had helped. Because of that I had been given permission to express some of the feelings for the family that had been suppressed for so long. Now I was in touch with five of the children, and had met four. Each one is important to me – they are special people who deserve respect and consideration. Their kindness and their acceptance have been greater than I had any hope of expecting. We are all now working together to try to trace the last of the family, Bridget or Bridie. I hope we find her. We have reason to believe that she emigrated to Australia . . .

Other titles published by Piatkus Books

Reincarnation: The Evidence
by Liz Hodgkinson

In *Reincarnation: The Evidence* medical journalist and author Liz Hodgkinson examines the part reincarnation plays in the major world religions, in spiritual healing, in past-life regression, hypnosis and psychiatry. She also investigates a number of fascinating case histories and then weighs up the arguments for and against reincarnation, leaving no stone unturned in her search for the truth. The result is a compelling read which presents both sides of the argument and finally leaves the reader to make up their own mind.

Karma and Reincarnation
by Dr Hiroshi Motoyama

A powerful and accessible book which will appeal to everyone who is interested in reincarnation and spiritual growth. *Karma and Reincarnation* is based on the work and experiences of Dr Hiroshi Motoyama, a scientist and Shinto priest with a worldwide following, who has awoken to states of consciousness that enable him to see beyond the limits of time and space. Using examples from his psychic experiences and work as a healer and guide, Dr Motoyama gives a clear explanation of the ongoing evolution of man. He shows that an understanding of karma, the law of cause and effect, and reincarnation will help us to dissolve the various karma − personal, marital and family, national and global − which continue to affect our daily lives.

Hypnosis Regression Therapy
and How It Can Help You
by Ursula Markham

In this helpful book, Ursula Markham, one of Britain's most respected hypnotherapists, answers many of the questions people have about hypnosis regression therapy. With the aid of case histories, she looks at the many types of problems that can be successfully overcome with hypnosis regression therapy and shows how you too can benefit. Problems which respond well include: anxiety and panic attacks; emotional problems; low self-esteem; stammering; depression; phobias; impotence; and weight problems. This authoritative book shows you how to increase your wellbeing, overcome your problems and create a happier and more fulfilling life.

The Power of Your Dreams
by Soozi Holbeche

In *The Power of Your Dreams* the well-known healer and dream therapist, Soozi Holbeche, uses examples from her own life and from her therapy sessions and dream workshops to explain how dreams have the power to prophesy, heal, guide and empower. She describes why we dream and what effect dreams can have on our waking life. Discover how easy it is to recall and interpret your dreams, work with nightmares, incubate dreams to solve problems, improve relationships and sexuality, learn from the sacred dreaming traditions of other cultures, and use your dreams as a pathway to the soul.

The Afterlife
by Jenny Randles and Peter Hough

The Afterlife is a fascinating investigation into what happens to us after we die. Should we believe the stories we hear about near-death experiences, out-of-body survival, reincarnation, ghostly hauntings and messages from beyond the grave? Does a part of us live on after death? Packed with an enthralling mixture of scientific facts, spine-chilling stories and photographic evidence, *The Afterlife* will help you to make up your own mind once and for all . . .

Jenny Randles and Peter Hough are both well respected researchers and writers in the paranormal field.

Transformed by the Light
by Dr Melvin Morse with Paul Perry

Millions of people throughout the world have had a near-death experience. In this fascinating and moving book, near-death researcher Melvin Morse and writer Paul Perry present a wealth of evidence from people who have returned from death after being *Transformed by the Light*. They show how the lives of people who return from the brink of death are usually changed for the better both spiritually and physically. These extraordinary revelations may permanently alter your views on death and dying.

For a free brochure with further information on our complete range of titles, please write to the following address. (Freepost is only available in the UK.)

Piatkus Books
Freepost 7 (WD 4504)
London W1E 4EZ

PIATKUS